TALES FROM TRACKSIDE

Barney Hall

with Ben White

SPORTS PUBLISHING L.L.C.

SportsPublishingLLC.com

Publishers: Peter L. Bannon and Joseph J. Bannon Sr.
Senior managing editor: Susan M. Moyer
Acquisitions editor: Lynnette Bogard
Developmental editor: Lynnette Bogard
Art director: K. Jeffrey Higgerson
Dust jacket design: Heidi Norsen
Interior layout: Kathryn R. Holleman
Photo editor: Erin Linden-Levy

Printed in the United States of America

Sports Publishing L.L.C.
804 North Neil Street
Champaign, IL 61820
Phone: 1-877-424-2665
Fax: 217-363-2073
SportsPublishingLLC.com

Library of Congress Cataloging-in-Publication Data

Hall, Barney.
    Barney Hall's tales from trackside / Barney Hall with Ben White.—1st ed.
        p. cm.
    ISBN 1-59670-007-6 (hardcover : alk. paper)
    1. Hall, Barney. 2. Sportscasters—United States—Anecdotes. 3. Stock car
racing. 4. NASCAR (Association) I. White, Ben, 1960- II. Title.

GV742.42.H34A3 2006
070.4'49796092—dc22

                            2006004293

I would like to dedicate this book to my mother,
Cindy Mazie Shumate.
Throughout many wonderful years together, she was my very best
friend and biggest supporter.

—BH

CONTENTS

ACKNOWLEDGMENTS

I have a lot of people to thank for their help and friendships over the years and there have been many.

I will start with Jim Foster, who was the "Boss Man" at Motor Racing Network for a lot of years. His support and encouragement is probably why I'm here today.

Likewise to the late Bill France Sr. and Bill France Jr., who put up with my mistakes on the air and made sure I learned from them, as well as John McMullen, who ran MRN for many years.

Thank you to Jack Arute, Mike Joy, Eli Gold, Joe Moore, and Alan Bestwick, some of the guys I've worked with in the MRN booth.

Also, a thank you to our pit and turn announcers, Mike Bagley, Dan Hubbard, Winston Kelley, Jim Phillips, Dave Moody, Adam Alexander, Jerry Punch, Ned Jarrett, Fred Armstrong and a dozen others. They've all helped me do a better job on the air and made us all sound good during our race broadcasts.

In the last few years, David Hyatt, our president and general manager of MRN, has really been a big reason I'm still doing this for a living. Thank you, David.

Thank you to all the drivers and crews who have allowed me their time, as well as for having confidence in me during interviews over the years.

Finally, a special thanks to Ben White for his help with the writing of this book. We've both had a great time talking and laughing and reliving all the old stories gathered together on these pages.

—Barney Hall

I would like to express a very sincere thank you to Barney Hall for allowing me to put his life and stories on paper. The friendship we've shared over the years, as well as the hours we have spent compiling the content for this book have been very special.

I would also like to thank Lynnette Bogard of Sports Publishing LLC for her interest and excitement concerning *Tales from Trackside*.

Finally, I'd like to thank my wife, Eva, and son, Aaron, for allowing me the many hours needed to complete this project. I sincerely appreciate your support and patience.

—Ben White

1

BORN AND RAISED IN ELKIN

I will readily admit my career as a motorsports broadcaster was about as likely to happen as jumping into a rocket and landing on the moon. I didn't grow up thinking I would be in the radio profession. You could say it just happened.

I've been quite content throughout my life with the slow pace that being from a mountain mill town in western North Carolina offers. My hometown is Elkin, North Carolina, a small crossroads community of about 9,000. Life is quiet and peaceful there, while the rest of the world is somewhere in either direction of Interstate 77 that passes just outside of town. Once on the exit ramp into Elkin, an entirely new world begins. It's a place where everyone knows everyone and a helping hand from a neighbor is just a phone call away. For me, it's the easy, slower pace that makes life so special.

Even from an early age, I never entertained the thought that such NASCAR stock car legends as Glen "Junior" Johnson, David Pearson or Cale Yarborough would someday become a few of the vast number of friends I would come to know in the sport. To routinely associate with racing celebrities has been very rewarding. But then again, I never thought I would be a part of an exciting sport such as NASCAR racing. Over the years, announcing NASCAR races has taken me all around the United States and to select parts of the world.

To this day, I continue to live in my hometown, and when I'm not on the road going to races, I spend a good bit of time on my deck, staring out at the beautiful Blue Ridge mountains off in the distance. What I enjoy the most is watching the deer come less than a hundred yards from the house, and there are usually four or five that come by at a time.

Even though other towns have grown a lot over the years, Elkin is still relatively small. I was born and raised there and haven't lived anywhere else, except for about five years that I spent in the Navy. I've just always loved Elkin because you kind of know everybody. The best part is that a traffic jam there is 10 cars, and you might have to a wait a while to get that many.

Having been an only child with no brothers and sisters to call on, I spent a great deal of time with my grandmother, Lillie Hall, when I was in grade school. I lived with my grandmother from the time I was about five or six years old until I was about eight or nine.

My mom, Mazie Shumate, and my stepfather, Bryce Shumate, moved to Charlottesville, Virginia, but I went there one weekend and didn't like the place at all. I cried and pitched a fit so I was able to go home and live with my grandmother. For a long time, I was closer to her than I was to my mother. In later years, it kind of went the other way. I figured they both raised me.

My father, Walter Peety, passed away when I was about two years old, and I really don't know much about him. My mother remarried in the mid-1930s to Bryce, and he died when I was about 18 or 19, just about the time I was getting ready to go into the Navy. My mother passed away on February 13, 2003, at the age of 88. I was very close to my mother in her later years, but I wasn't very close to my stepfather, because we didn't get along that well. I guess I was kind of a mule-headed kid who was strong-willed. We had a couple of run-ins and he tanned my butt a couple of times. As a kid, I got a lot of whippings, and I'd say I deserved most of them. My grandmother didn't do that to me too much. If I got a whipping from her, I really deserved it.

I remember my relatives talking about NASCAR racing as a teenager. They would often gather around front porches or dinner tables and talk about such drivers as Red Byron, the Flock brothers—Tim, Fonty, and Bob—and Curtis Turner, to name only a few. NASCAR racing was something exciting for a small town with very little going on. It gave people something to talk about. Most of my uncles and close relatives were more or less race fans back in the early days of stock car racing. I guess hearing them talk about going to the old dirt track races in the open fields around Wilkesboro (North Carolina) and places like that made me want to go.

People have asked me if I remember the first race I ever attended, and I tell them I do very clearly. I slipped off one time and went to a dirt track race in Jonesville, North Carolina, a little town close to Elkin. A couple of guys I was in school with and I walked about five miles to go to a race. We could hear the cars and see the dust rising up long before we got to the track. I think I was in the seventh or eighth grade at the time. That was actually before NASCAR was formed, but there were all kinds of small racing sanctions and clubs springing up here and there after World War II. NASCAR was formed in February of 1948 by William H.G. "Bill" France, the man who organized stock car racing and developed it with the idea of making it into a nationally known sport. After decades of racing, it has finally been accepted along with professional football, baseball, and basketball.

As I got closer to that track, I remember thinking how amazed I was at seeing the makeshift race track in the distance. So much was going on, it was difficult for my young eyes to take it all in. It had a wooden fence, and it didn't really do much good to look through the slats because the dust was so bad. So I climbed up the outside of the fence in turn three and sat on the edge. I was sitting there watching them go at it pretty hard up front for the lead. I'll never forget when one of the cars kicked a big clod of dirt from the track right about the

During a special press conference in the late 1960s, Hall interviews NASCAR founder Bill France, Sr. It was one of many hundreds of interviews Hall conducted over the past 45 years of racing. *Motorsports Images & Archives. Used with permission.*

time I got positioned on that fence. That clod of dirt was as big as a pretty good-sized turnip and it hit me right between the eyes and knocked me off the fence. I really didn't know what had hit me, and I fell and rolled down into a nearby creek. So that was my very first introduction to big league stock car racing.

I discovered, too, that I enjoyed other sports, as most high school boys do. They were the normal, more mainstream sports, like football, baseball, and basketball. Even though I was rather small in size, football really appealed to me. That is until I figured out there was a difference between running the ball and being caught by the defense while running the ball.

I went out for everything. I played some basketball, and I enjoyed several sports, but football was the sport I liked the most. I wished that I was bigger, because I really liked playing. I played first-string tackle for a couple of years. Back then, you would go to high school in the eighth grade. They didn't have a junior varsity team. The coaches let you dress out, and if you were a halfway decent player and showed you could hold your own, they would put you in the game. The last two years I played, I was in the backfield at the position of tailback. I was pretty quick, and being small helped in that department, I guess. I wasn't that great of an athlete, but I thought I was as good as everyone else.

In my senior year my football career took a rather unexpected turn. My ambition to play football got squashed, and I mean literally.

There was one boy on the opposing team who was about the size of King Kong, and he was a bad dude. I was running the ball and I saw him coming at me. I probably weighed 129 or 130 pounds, and he had to weigh maybe 240. He hit me, and he was bad about stepping on players. He put his foot on my hand, and that was when they had the real football cleats. He tore my hand up pretty good, and after that I thought I really didn't need to be getting hurt anymore. Football was fun, but I decided I wasn't all that crazy about pain. It was fine until somebody really big tackled me, then I was ready to do something else.

As far as my high school education was concerned, I found myself in a rather unique position. Like most teenage boys, attending classes didn't appeal to me, and I looked for any way to get away from chalkboards and classrooms that I could find. The offer to attend school part-time and work part-time was too good to turn down.

During my senior year, they had a program called Diversified Education, in which students could attend school for half a day and work the other half. I worked in a textile mill; the lifeblood of the town of Elkin was textiles. The company I worked for was Chatham Manufacturing, and my job was making blankets. The company is still in existence today.

With cars blazing by below, Hall is in his broadcast position in turn one at Martinsville (Virginia) Speedway in the early 1970s.
Motorsports Images & Archives. Used with permission.

If you lived in Elkin back then, you either worked in the furniture plant or you made blankets. I worked in about every department they had, from the weave room to the dye house. I did it all, but I knew I really didn't want to be a textile worker.

When I finally left Elkin, I guess you could say it was to find myself. I wanted to look for a career away from all those clacking sounds of textile machines and thread spinners. I knew that just wasn't what I wanted to do. So when I graduated from high school in 1950, I went to Baltimore, Maryland, and took a job with Glennel-Martin Aircraft where I worked as a riveter. We built seaplanes, the P5-M1s for the Navy. I enjoyed that, because I had always been fascinated with flying.

Glennel-Martin lost some government contracts to another company and had to downsize, so from there I went to work at Maryland Dry Dock as a riveter building ships. But that didn't pan out very well, either. They, too, lost some government contracts, and I, like so many others, was back on the street again. I next went to work for Chevrolet at Fisher Bodies.

I finally went into the Navy in December of 1952, and when I came out at the end of 1957, I wasn't sure what I wanted to do. I worked doing a little bit of everything, and that even included building houses. But my desire to be as perfect as possible meant I wasn't very fast, and that profession fell by the wayside.

While I was trying to make up my mind about what I wanted to do, my uncle, who worked as a brick mason, offered me a job mixing cement. He taught me how to lay brick. I still lay brick and do a lot of that kind of stuff now when I have the time for my own projects at my cabin. I was just never quick enough to make a living at it. Where someone else might lay brick in 20 minutes, it would take me two hours. Brick laying is back-breaking work. It wasn't the career I was hoping for, but it was a job. Over the years, I've learned to be a pretty good carpenter, and I built my own house and a cabin in the mountains.

I also later returned to work at Chatham Manufacturing Co., a place I really didn't want to be. The job provided a paycheck, but absolutely no chance to rise any higher in the company.

I knew there had to be something better for me out there somewhere.

2

THE BRAVE AVIATOR

From the time I was a teenager, I've enjoyed a love for aviation. Later in life, I often put that love for flying to good use by piloting friends to races on the NASCAR schedule over the past four decades. I think of my time in the sky as the absolute perfect getaway, because flying to me is so peaceful.

My personal path toward becoming a pilot was rather unconventional, to say the least.

As a junior in high school in the spring of 1949, I shared an interest in powered model airplanes with a friend named Hubert Whittington. Hubert's dad owned the local furniture store in town, and the two of us became fast friends. We spent many hours building airplanes from balsa wood and enjoyed flying them. We bought them with money from odd part-time jobs around the furniture store or doing things wherever we could pick up a few dollars.

Some of the model airplanes that we built came with engines. Supposedly they were radio-controlled, but the definition of remote control in those days was to have a little device in it to keep it running, and you would fly it on a wire around and around in a circle over your head.

We occasionally thumbed through the want ads of the local *Elkin Tribune* newspaper to see if anyone had model airplanes or parts for sale. One particular ad caught our attention. The ad in the paper said a J4 airplane was for sale in Greensboro, North Carolina, which was about 45 minutes away by car. They were high back then, and the price for this one was $250. So Hubert and I decided to go and look at it.

When we got to Greensboro, our mouths dropped when we discovered it was a real airplane. We sort of looked at one another, and before the end of the day, we had bought ourselves a real airplane. Neither one of us could fly it. We got the guy who ran the airfield there in Elkin to fly it back for us. His name was Grey Brown.

I remember Grey—or Mr. Brown to us boys then—ground looped it when he flew it back in. I also remember it had a real narrow landing gear on it. He told us he wouldn't teach us to fly in it because he said, "That airplane would kill us all!" The thing sat there at the airfield for a whole summer.

Every other day or so, I would ride out to the airfield and stare at our new investment. I would piddle with the engine, shine it up or just sit behind the controls from time to time. But to have it was about as useless as a candle without a wick. We could stare at it and dream of flying it, but that was about the extent of it. When I did finally get it going, I would ride in it up and down the runway, just to taxi it around. I would raise and lower the tail on it with a control stick it had in it. I did have about two hours of training with an instructor in a J3 Cub, and I knew all the principles of flying.

I woke up one morning with an idea that I couldn't shake. I called Hubert and told him I was coming by to pick him up and that we were going to the airfield.

We got there and we were sitting around in the plane. I told Hubert that I was tired of just driving it up and down the runway. We had an airplane and nobody to teach us how to fly it.

I said to Hubert, "You'd better get out, because I'm going to take it around the field." Hubert piped up and said, "Are you kidding?" I said, "No, I think I can fly this thing." To that, Hubert said, "Well, hell, if you're crazy enough to do it, I'm crazy enough to go with you."

I told him I was serious, and he said he was, too. I gave it power, and the two of us took off down the runway.

I admit I had more trouble taking off than I did landing. Not being used to the rudder pedals, I was all over the runway. But I came back in and made the best landing I've ever made in my life.

Once the two of us got back on the ground, we exchanged smiles, partly because of what we had accomplished and partly because we hadn't been killed in the process.

From the moment my wheels finally left the runway, I was hooked on flying. I found myself flying virtually everywhere for the next two and a half years and collected more than a hundred hours of flying time. When I needed to go somewhere, I would just jump in it and take off.

All the while, I had never given any thought to getting a pilot's license. I was doing just fine without one. Then one day, fate finally caught up with me as I was attempting a landing. It was the day I thought my flying had come to a permanent end.

I was flying back into the Elkin airport one day, and as you might expect, it was a rather small airport. I was coming back in and I landed head-on in the path of another airplane. I never thought about landing up wind or down wind. That never crossed my mind. I saw this airplane coming in from the other end of the runway. He pulled up and went around.

When we were putting our airplane in the hangar, this guy came up, and he was livid! I didn't know who he was, and when he asked to see my license, I told him I didn't have one. "Were you flying that Bonanza we almost flew into?" he asked me. I told him I was and he said, "On top of being an idiot, you're a smart ass, too."

He said he was J.A. Pilker, head of the Charlotte Division of the Civil Aeronautics Administration (now known as the Federal Aviation

Administration) and he was in charge of the whole district. I thought to myself, "Oh, Lord. I'm in real trouble. My flying days are over."

When he said, "Let me see your license," I told him that I was serious, that I didn't have one. I told him that I had been flying for about two and a half years and he said, "I ain't believing this."

Pilker shook his head from side to side and he asked, "How often do you fly?" I said, "About every day if the weather's good." He finally said, "Well, if you ain't got a license, I can't take it. Apparently, you boys are flying on a shoestring. So I'll tell you what I'm going to do. I'm going to recommend that you go to Statesville, North Carolina and get linked up with the Miller boys. They are licensed instructors. Go down there and let them check you out and write you out a student license."

Pilker turned to walk away from us and stopped and asked, "Have you ever been to Statesville?" I just laughed and said, "Yeah, all the time." He said, "You mean you fly across country? Do you have a radio in that cracker box? How do you navigate?" I told him, "No, we don't have a radio. It was supposed to have one in it but it didn't when we bought it. I just go about 10 miles out toward Highway 421 and there's two silos out at this dairy farm and that's where I know to turn and go right into Statesville."

Then he said, "Go to see the Miller boys, and I better not catch you again without a license," and he walked out of the hangar. I said, "Yes sir," and Hubert nodded, still too scared to talk.

Two weeks later, I flew into Statesville and met the Miller boys. After some test runs, I walked out with a student license. I sometimes question why we didn't end up in the obituary section of the *Elkin Tribune* in those days. We had plenty of reasons to be there.

When I finally did ride with an instructor, I learned right quick that I didn't know anything about flying. Hubert and I were real lucky we didn't wind up dead. I quickly discovered some of my methods went against the rules of physics.

When I got ready to turn one way or the other in that old airplane, I was doing it all wrong. You're supposed to use the stick and the rudder and coordinate the two. You lay the stick over to the left and you give it a little rudder pedal and you kind of go into a bank and make the turn. Before I knew any better, I would just kick the left rudder pedal and let the tail skid around. But that can put you into a stall and a spin, and down you go.

I had been flying like that, and the instructor I was with saw what I was doing. He asked me if I flew like that all the time, and I told him I did. He said, "Let me show you one day what's going to happen to you if you keep doing that." He kicked the rudder and held it, and the airplane vibrated real badly and it rolled over and went into a spin. I thought I was going to die of a heart attack. He let it turn about three times and then pulled out of it. At that point, I was probably as white as a sheet. I'm just thankful I never got in trouble doing that because I wouldn't have been able to recover from it. I had somebody looking out for me, that's for sure.

So that's the story of how I began flying. But if you did today what I did when I started flying, the FAA would fine you $10,000. And the only thing you would be flying from then on would be a kite.

3

THE MOVE TO RADIO

People have asked me how I got involved in radio, and I've always said it was simply by accident. It all started through a friend I met in high school, named Johnny Hunter. He had a part-time job cleaning the control room at WIFM Radio in Elkin. His voice was pleasant and even-toned, and the station manager, Gene Smith, recognized his gift. He began letting Johnny read non-sponsored newscasts and doing public service announcements on the air.

After all of the jobs I had attempted, I was impressed that Johnny was doing something exciting rather than the usual mundane things around town like pumping gas, boxing and delivering groceries, and those boring plant jobs. I wanted to do something better than that.

Johnny was a big hero of mine, and I listened to him every chance I got. To be on the radio back then was a big deal and I thought that I would like to try it. I had always listened while I was growing up to shows like *The Bob Hope Show* and *The Red Skelton Show* and stuff like that. That was our entertainment in the 1930s and '40s because TV wasn't around yet. I had always liked radio and all of the shows that were on it.

After Johnny graduated from high school in 1957, he began working full time at the radio station. Sadly, only a few months passed before he was killed in a car accident. I had had relatives pass away during my lifetime, but I guess you could say my first real experience with the death of someone close to me was Johnny. I got word of his death when I was just about ready to leave the Navy.

In early 1958, the thought of working in radio surfaced again. It was through a local bowling tournament I was involved in. Another friend I met through Johnny was also in the tournament and he would play a key role in my future career. That friend was Gene Smith, the station manager at WIFM radio.

I used to bowl in a league that had the old duck pins. The ball was about the size of a grapefruit, and the pins were much smaller than the regulation-sized pins.

The Elkin radio station sponsored the local bowling team. Gene bowled on the team and asked me if I knew where he could find a good radio announcer. I said I did, and he asked who it was. I said, "That person is me!" He asked me if I had experience in radio, and of course I lied like a dog. I said I did, and he immediately asked where.

My mind was working 150 miles an hour, so I thought of a buddy I was stationed with in Okinawa in the Armed Forces radio station. His job was to file records for the station and I had been up there a lot of times just hanging out with him. I said, "I did some stuff for Armed Forces radio when I was in the service."

Finally, Gene said he would audition me and that he might give me a job. He also told me the job paid $45 per week, and that was about what I was making for two weeks at the time. So obviously, that was very good money to me.

I called in sick to the plant that next Monday and raced down to the radio station for an interview. Gene handed me several pieces of paper. One of them was a Sunbeam Bread commercial that was routinely read over the air. Another was about two or three minutes of news off of the old Associated Press news machine. A third was a commercial for the local Belk department store.

I look back and laugh at all of that now, but there was nothing funny about it then. Things didn't go as well as I had hoped, and I thought I was finished before I ever got started.

Gene told me to go in the studio and read all of those pages for him. I was so nervous you could hear the paper shaking through the microphone because it was rattling so badly in my hands. I called Sunbeam Bread everything but Sunbeam. I was so embarrassed I just finally quit. Gene was laughing the whole time and finally he came in there and said, "You lying rascal! You've never even been in a radio station have you?" I said, "Yeah, I've been in one, but I've never announced before."

He told me I had a good voice and said, "Why don't you take these two commercials and the news sheets home and just get in a room by yourself and read them." He gave me what is known as a wire recorder, something that was available before portable tape recorders came out, and showed me how to run it. I've still got that wire recording and I still listen to it every now and then. My voice didn't sound a whole lot different then than what it sounds like now. I did great when there was no one around, but if someone were watching me, I would get torn all to pieces. I stayed that way for a long time.

I went home pretty dejected that day. But I did what Gene told me to do and continued practicing and was granted a second tryout. I improved each time I tried it, and was doing much better than when I suffered the disaster that took place a few days earlier.

Gene gave me the job for two weeks and let me read unsponsored newscasts, just like he had done with Johnny before he died. After three days had passed, Gene came in and said, "Congratulations. You've got the job."

I guess you could say I continued to get better at announcing and became a lot more comfortable behind the microphone. It took a while, but with more on-air time, I felt more at ease with the radio job.

Anyone who has worked for a small radio station knows you have to wear many hats doing many different jobs. One of mine was to go through the daily mail and sort it. Within those letters were press releases that also served as invitations from NASCAR to represent the station at local races in the area.

I had no idea then that they were also invitations for a lifelong career in the sport.

4

THE FIRST TRIP TO THE PITS

The year I began spinning records, perfecting commercials and reading the news at WIFM radio, NASCAR was in its 10th year of existence. And the only superspeedway on NASCAR's schedule in 1958 was the Darlington Raceway in Darlington, South Carolina. The track had been hosting the prestigious Southern 500 since Labor Day of 1950 and had gained a reputation for being a rather treacherous mile and a third of asphalt. The rest of the races on the often-makeshift schedule consisted of dirt and asphalt short tracks around the country as well as races on the sands of Daytona Beach, Florida.

Daytona International Speedway would not be added until the next year. The announcement that it was being built came in 1955, but it wasn't completed until four years later. Yes, there was Indianapolis Motor Speedway, the famed two-and-a-half-mile oval that officially opened on August 12, 1909. But for the majority of the 20th century, it was strictly used for open-wheel Indy car races.

A few stock car tire tests had taken place there in the early 1960s with drivers Marvin Panch, Lloyd Ruby and Glenn "Fireball" Roberts, to name a few, but Tony Hulman, the track's longtime owner, wanted no part of stock cars racing on his race track. It would break a longstanding tradition of only open-wheel cars taking to the relatively flat, rectangular-shaped track.

A superspeedway in Daytona was simply Bill France's dream. Standing six feet five inches, he beamed from ear to ear once Daytona International Speedway finally had fans passing through the track's gates after years of searching for financing and cutting through legal red tape. His vision has paid off well. Over five decades of racing have brought untold financial wealth and economic success to Volusia County, Florida. Come to think of it, that success has been enjoyed by all areas that have hosted NASCAR events.

Many of the other superspeedways, such as Charlotte, Rockingham, Dover, Michigan, and Talladega, were built throughout the 1960s and remain on the schedule today.

How France chose to make Daytona Beach the stock car racing capital of the world was quite by accident. France had already entertained the possibility of forming a racing sanction and had chosen Miami as his place to call home. He and his wife, Annie B. France, were relocating there from Washington, D.C. in 1934 and stopped to visit relatives and spend the night in Ormond Beach, a small surfside town about 25 miles north of Daytona. The Frances fell in love with the area and decided to settle there in Volusia County, Florida, instead of Miami, some 350 miles south. He opened a gas station in Daytona Beach that also served as an informal headquarters for NASCAR in the very early stages of its existence.

When France finally got NASCAR up and running, he had a small staff of public relations representatives who promoted his idea that radio was a perfect tool for exposing NASCAR to the general public. I often received NASCAR press releases announcing upcoming events at tracks around North Carolina.

Houston Lawing and a guy named Bob Pope served as NASCAR's public relations and media representatives in the late 1950s. Their job was to get people to go to races at tracks like Martinsville, Virginia,

While working as a track announcer at Bristol Motor Speedway in the early 1960s, Hall introduces National Football League great Johnny Unitas just prior to race time. Unitas enjoyed much of his success while with the Baltimore Colts.

Motorsports Images & Archives. Used with permission.

and North Wilkesboro, North Carolina, and other local tracks they were using in the area. And they asked us to use the radio station to keep the public informed about NASCAR events.

At the bottom of the press release was a line or two about what type of racing they were promoting and the location of the track. Also at the bottom of the page was a line urging newspapers and radio stations to write or call for more information. I would call and ask for a couple of tickets every now and then, and I would offer them to a few of my buddies. That number of tickets increased as time passed.

In time, I was starting to do some sports at the radio station, and along with that, I would read stock car racing reports and race results. I started doing interviews with drivers, and luckily by that time, portable tape recorders were just becoming available.

I decided it might boost WIFM's listening audience if I played some of my interviews with drivers during some of those race reports I announced during the day. The listeners always wanted to know what was going on with the drivers, just like they do today.

I remember there was a race coming up at Martinsville, Virginia, in the spring of 1958, and I made arrangements for credentials. It was my first trip to a race track garage area, and it brought back that same excitement I felt during that first race at Jonesboro many years earlier.

The first driver I ever interviewed was Buddy Baker. He is the son of NASCAR champion Buck Baker and the winner of 19 NASCAR races during a driving career that spanned over 20 seasons.

I drove to Martinsville to talk to Baker, but I didn't know him personally. I had seen him race, but that was it. He is about six feet four inches tall, and I'm about five foot seven. I walked up to him and asked if I could talk with him for a minute, and he agreed that the time was good.

Now Baker has a little bit of a lisp, and he's very self-conscious about it. I didn't know that at the time. I asked him a question and he answered and was kind of lisping a little bit. I thought he was pulling my leg. The next question I asked, I kind of did the same to him. He stepped back and got real red in the face. He looked at me hard and said, "Boy, if you don't quit doing that, I'm going to stick that microphone where you're going to have trouble talking to anybody!" He turned around and walked off, and it really scared me to death. I didn't know what had happened to make him mad. I really didn't.

I mentioned the incident to some friends I found in the pits and they replied, "Don't you know Baker has a slight speech impediment? He's very sensitive about it." I told them I didn't, and they said I'd better not do that anymore. And I never did.

Through my connections with friends in the broadcast business, I had offers to do part-time track public address announcing at several tracks on the circuit over the next couple of years. I found it to be quite rewarding and it also offered me more exposure to the drivers and teams. An exciting world was opening up right before my eyes.

Ted Webb, an announcer with NBC, heard me and liked my style, I guess. Ted used to do a lot of stuff for the Daytona 500 broadcasts on the side with WNDB, the radio station in Daytona. He heard me doing some P.A. announcing at some other tracks. Ted told me they were going to hire two announcers for the old Daytona 500 network. He wanted me to come to Daytona and audition, but I hardly had enough money to get there and back home. I was just being honest with him and told him I just didn't have the money. I think he had already made up his mind he was going to hire me, to tell you the truth.

I called him and told him I just couldn't come and why. Ted agreed to send me $100 to come down to Florida. He said he would put me on the air the Tuesday before Speedweeks. They started then and ran all week. He said, "We'll put you on the Twin 125s [qualifying races] and we'll pay you the $100 either way." So I stayed out of work and went to Daytona.

I felt very fortunate to get the job because there were quite a few top-notch announcers going for those positions. Some were so good they were a little bit intimidating.

There were about 20 guys who wanted the two jobs, and one of those was Chris Economaki. Ray Melton was another, as well as

Sammy Bland. They hired me and another guy I had never heard of named Bob McGinley. I'm really not sure what happened to Bob. I don't think he stayed in the sport very long.

Ted put me out in turn four about eight steps off the race track on a scaffold about five feet high. I thought, "This is great, I'll be right here close to the action." I didn't realize and the people who hired me didn't realize how dangerous it really was. This was in the Daytona 500 in 1960, the second Daytona 500 ever run.

They ran a lap or two and I was shaking and nervous and I had a piece of paper in front of me because I didn't know the drivers that well. I thought, "You've blown this. They're not going to hire you."

After about the first 10 laps, everything that happened in the race happened right in front of me. There were all kinds of wrecks and cars landing on top of each other. There were some that turned upside down and caught fire. After that, I forgot about being scared and just reported what I saw. I guess they liked what they heard, because I've been doing a race broadcast ever since.

Another help to me was Hal Hamrick, a gentleman who had also worked at the Elkin station. He left to go to work as public relations director for what was then known as Bristol International Raceway that opened in 1961. Hal asked me if I would like to come up to Bristol and work as a back-up announcer to Bob Montgomery in the booth. Bob was the chief announcer back then, and some tracks organized their own radio broadcasts. He was someone highly respected in both radio circles as well as racing circles.

Unlike what I told my first station manager, I told Hal the truth and said I had never done that kind of announcing before. He said to me, "Bob isn't going to let you talk much, but if he needs a break every now and then, he'll call on you to help. For five minutes every so often, you can announce to the fans inside the track."

From there, I started listening intently to a couple of my broadcast heroes and tried to pattern myself after them. I admit they were hard acts to follow.

Hall (left) is shown with fellow announcers Ken Squier (center) and Jack Arute. Both Squier and Arute worked with Motor Racing Network in the mid-1970s.
Motorsports Images & Archives. Used with permission.

Bob Montgomery was the first announcer I remember in the early 1960s who brought dignity to the sport. He didn't scream and holler and try to make things bigger than they really were. A lot of the early race broadcasts often only had one turn guy, and Winston Kelley's father, Earl Kelley, worked with them in those days.

I tried to do a lot of stuff like Bob did, especially talking in a normal tone. But then if something exciting happened, I always thought if you are a good announcer, you can get excited without screaming at people. Montgomery was one of my heroes.

Another person I patterned myself after is Ken Squier. Ken was the guy who taught me a lot about being meticulous about detail. I never was much of a statistics man. I like to look out through a booth window or work in a turn and really describe who was beating on whom or which driver was running where and passing and moving up. But at the same time, I liked Ken's style and copied a little bit of that.

I've got some of those old tapes, and we did mumble and stumble and fumble a lot back then, but nobody thought a lot about it. There weren't that many announcers who had done that many races. The race fans wanted to hear it, even if you were half right on reporting something. You couldn't do that today, though. Race fans follow racing so closely now and they pick up on any mistakes you make. That's why it's so hard for guys to break into covering races on the radio. You can't afford to put somebody out in a turn or any position on a national network and let them stand out in a turn or work pit road and have them fumble and made mistakes. There's no place to learn this other than doing public announcing at race tracks. There's no way to go out in a turn and do it on a network because there are no small networks anymore. Race broadcasting now is totally different than what it was 45 years ago. There's really no comparison.

I admit I still listen to those old tapes from time to time and will occasionally cringe at the sound of them. Compared to the polished work that MRN Radio produces today, some of them sound rather rough. But still, they're fun to listen to and they bring back many, many memories.

5

MEETING JUNIOR

F lying airplanes has always offered me a great many opportunities to meet various people within NASCAR. Even today, I never turn down anyone who wants to talk about aviation or occasional flights with drivers if they are ever offered to me. I'm simply fascinated by going from one place to another through wide-open blue skies.

I can credit airplanes as the foundation for how I first met Junior Johnson, which was about 1951 or '52. I found myself hanging around the Elkin airport one afternoon with my flight instructor and friend, Grey Brown. That day, Grey had a special student driving up from Wilkes County with some of his friends. It was Junior, a part-time race car driver who had already made a name for himself in the North Carolina mountains as a moonshiner.

I remember those sunny afternoons when Junior first tried his hand at flying. How he gained his short-lived ownership of an airplane proved to be quite an interesting story.

Junior sold a guy about $300 worth of moonshine, and the guy couldn't pay him. On top of that, the guy got caught making some of his own moonshine and got put in jail for about a year or so. He called Junior from jail and said, "I can't pay for the moonshine, but I've got an airplane. If you want it, you can go down and get it and sell it, and it will probably bring about what I owe you."

So Junior suddenly had a reason to learn to fly and hired Grey to teach him. Remember, this is the same guy who wouldn't teach Hubert and me to fly our airplane years earlier because, as he said, "it would kill us all."

Grey went down and brought the airplane back to Elkin and started giving Junior flying lessons in it. The plane Junior got through the moonshine deal gone bad was a Tailorcraft.

Each time Junior would show up for a lesson, he would come out there with six or seven of his buddies. They were a wild crowd. They would be sitting on a wooden fence waiting on Grey to show up so Junior could take the lessons. Junior would say, "Boys, we're going to run a foot race to the hangar over there for $5 dollars apiece. So get your money out." Three or four of them jumped up and threw $5 down on the ground. He would count to three and they would take off and they'd all leave Junior behind, because he was pretty hefty in those days.

But Junior would wait until they almost got to the building and he would turn around and come back halfway. He'd beat them back, pick up the money, and put it in his pocket. They wouldn't say a word. He would just tell them how dumb they were, and they would go on.

I was there one day visiting Grey, and Junior was there. He had been taking lessons for a month or so. Junior started talking to me about flying and about racing and whatever. He had several hours of flying time by then, and Grey told me he thought Junior was going to make a pretty good pilot.

I was out there another afternoon, and it was the day Grey was going to let him solo and give him a student license. They were going to go around the field one more time and Grey was going to get out and let Junior fly by himself.

They came back in, and Grey got out and Junior took off. He got about 200 feet in the air and the engine quit. We saw the plane going down, and we all hopped off the fence and started running to where we thought the plane was going to go down. We didn't know what Junior had crashed into. We were afraid he had ended up in the lake at the end of the runway.

When we got out there, you could see that the airplane was okay and it was sitting out there in the pasture. What had happened was he was trying to get it down, and he caught the rear tail wheel on a fence. That had slowed it down and stood it on its nose, but the plane wasn't hurt all that bad. We didn't see Junior for a few seconds, and all of a sudden here he came running wide open on foot. We all said, "Junior, what happened?" But he didn't say a word. He just kept on going and went over and got in his car and sped off. He never flew that airplane again. He told Grey he could have it or do whatever he wanted to do with it, but he was not going to have anything to do with that airplane. So that's as close as Junior came to getting his pilot's license.

I actually flew the plane several times after that, but I don't know whatever happened to it. The best part of Junior's flying lessons was how we struck up a close friendship that has lasted over 50 years.

Some of NASCAR's truest, most interesting stories center around Junior Johnson. He learned to drive a pickup truck around the back roads of Wilkes County when he was 13 so he could help his dad in the moonshine business. He later used that talent behind the wheel of race cars and won an impressive number of NASCAR events as a driver. Once finished with winning races, he retired in 1966 to become one of the most successful team owners in history. He fielded cars that won six NASCAR championships with drivers Cale Yarborough in 1976, 1977 and 1978 and Darrell Waltrip in 1981, 1982 and 1985. For decades, his cars were occupied by some of the very best drivers in the business, collecting a total of 139 wins before selling his team to former driver Brett Bodine in 1995.

I've interviewed Junior countless times over the past four decades, gaining a huge variety of answers. But Junior never was one to give out a great deal of information any time he spoke. Junior was, and still is to this day, very soft spoken and sort of close to the vest as far as answers go. But he's always been that way. When he blew an engine during a race, you'd ask him what happened and he'd say, "It blowed up." If he blew a tire and hit the wall, he might say, "Bad tar," meaning tire. He would tell what you needed to know, but he would not give you a great deal of information. You'd have to sort of fish the answers out of him, then he would explain a little bit more but not a whole lot.

I liked watching Johnson weave through traffic on the race track when he drove. He always had that smoothness about him, especially when he was in tight packs of cars. But Junior wouldn't stay there for long and would often be the guy everyone else was chasing. That was especially true in 1963 when he won seven races, finished in the top five 13 times and top 10 14 times. He drove a solid white No. 3 Chevrolet for Ray Fox and went out and kicked everybody's butt with it. If he didn't win, he was right on the back bumper of the guy who did. Junior was a great race car driver, there's no doubt about that. He wasn't afraid to mix it up with anybody.

Actually, driving on a race track may have been easy for him considering all of his moonshine running on all those winding, dark mountain roads. It takes some true skill to drive a mountain road fast and not end up off the edge somewhere. Junior could handle a race car, and he proved that by winning so many races. He is tied with Ned Jarrett with 50 victories, and he's told me that if he had known it was a tie, he would have raced a little bit longer to get 51.

He really had even more success as a team owner than as a driver. His cars were always top of the line with top-flight drivers in them, like Cale Yarborough, Bobby Allison, Lee Roy Yarbrough, Charlie Glotzbach, and Darrell Waltrip, to name a few. And Junior was pretty good at building engines and building race cars. He knew how to make 'em go fast and knew what it took to win. But he also knew how to bend the rules as far as he could bend them without actually breaking them. And I guess there were a few times he may have crossed that line, but everyone has bent the rules a little. It's always been said the rule book can have several interpretations. That still goes on with some of the crew chiefs today.

Junior is one of the most colorful characters in the entire history of NASCAR, and I've truly enjoyed our friendship over the years.

For a good many mountain folk, making and running moonshine out of the North Carolina mountains was simply a way of life, and in some remote parts, it can still be found if you know who to ask, just like it was 60 years ago. Everyone was making it in the 1930s and '40s, even some of those who filled the church pews on Sunday mornings. Many offering plates were filled with money collected from illegal liquor.

Moonshiners in the North Carolina, Georgia, and Virginia mountains were good at making it, running it, and selling it. Growing corn paid off a lot more in moonshine than it did at the local farmers market. For some folks, it was simply the difference between eating and starving to death.

Peaches, apples, and cherries acted as a great way to flavor the mixture, but many preferred clear liquor to do their own mixing and chasing.

Making sure shipments were delivered on time meant using special cars that had been heavily modified to conceal and transport the goods. But the most important piece of the puzzle came with the person behind the steering wheel. The driver had to be both smart and fearless, especially on those winding mountain roads that rarely featured guardrails. They had to keep their cars from going into the rocky, tree-lined terrain below, or they'd lose the load and maybe their lives.

When it came to running moonshine, Johnson was one of the best drivers there was and knew where every dip and every hairpin turn was that lay in the asphalt or mountain dirt road.

So it seemed like a natural progression for Johnson to join NASCAR as a driver and take to the high-banked tracks like Daytona and Darlington as well as a variety of short tracks around the country.

After all, he learned the hard way how to drive fast. One minor slip meant certain prison time. Junior never made a mistake behind the wheel and never got caught running it. The only time he did get caught was during a surprise still raid that caused him to spend the majority of 1958 in prison. Had he not tripped over a barbwire fence that dark night as he ran away, he wouldn't have gotten caught.

Johnson's father, Robert Glen Johnson, Sr., made and sold his fair share of moonshine over the years, passing the craft on to his two sons, Junior and Fred. Not the type to put all of his eggs in one basket, Junior's dad had many stills going in various locations at the same time. So as early as Junior could remember, the sight of jugs and wooden crates were as common around the home as a pair of overalls or a plow.

I remember one story that was shared with me concerning Junior's family moonshine days when he and older brother Fred were very young.

I didn't get this from Junior. It was told to me several years ago by an old retired revenuer who was once assigned to find and arrest Junior's dad.

I was sitting in a local fast food restaurant in Elkin when a stranger approached me and introduced himself. He knew who I was and was aware that I knew Junior. He told me he once worked with the state looking for moonshiners, and he once had a funny encounter with Junior and his brother Fred when they were young boys back in the late 1930s.

According to the man, both had been playing in the front yard when he and his partner drove up at the Johnson home there in Wilkes County, North Carolina.

The revenuer told me during our conversation that they knew Junior's daddy was making moonshine all over the place and had chased him many times, but they could never catch him. They knew he was up in the woods somewhere but he had always stayed one step ahead of them. As I was listening, I thought to myself how that was the case with all good moonshiners. They knew how to outsmart the government boys.

Well, the revenuer told me he got out of the car that day and walked over to Junior and Fred. He said he squatted down and smiled and tried to be friendly with them.

He said, "Hello, boys. It looks like you both are having a lot fun playing." Fred looked up and said, "Yes sir, we sure are."

The revenuer then said, "Well, listen, I'm looking for your daddy. Would either one of you happen to know where I could find him? I have something I need to talk with him about."

Fred piped up and said, "Yes sir, but our daddy said I should never tell anybody where he is. Not ever!"

The revenue agent wasn't happy with that answer and said, "Come on, now. You can tell me just this one time, can't you?"

Fred then said, "Well, naw sir. Our daddy said we should never tell anybody where he is, and he meant it."

The revenue agent said he stood up and his partner reached in his wallet and got two five-dollar bills out and handed them to him. The revenue agent then said, "I'll tell you what I'm gonna do. I'm going to give both you boys five dollars each if you'll tell me where he is. You know, five dollars will buy a whole lot of candy or soda pop."

He said that Junior and Fred looked at one another in a long stare but didn't say anything, as if they were really giving the offer some thought. Finally, Junior looked up at the agent and said, "OK, give us the money, and I'll tell you where our daddy is."

Fred was sitting there and nodded in agreement.

The revenue agent said, "Oh, I can't do that. I need to find your daddy and talk to him first. Then I'll give you the money after I get back."

Knowing there were several men up on the mountain posted around the at the still with loaded shot guns, Junior hung his head in disappointment and said, "You'd better go ahead and give us the money now, 'cause if you go up to where my daddy is, you ain't coming back."

Junior showed that even back then he was a good businessman.

6

A FRIEND IN FIREBALL

Every era of NASCAR history seems to feature one superstar who stands out above the rest, someone who seems larger than life. That person in the early 1960s was Fireball Roberts.

The newspaper reporters and radio broadcasters who covered him that remain in the sport today often refer to Roberts as "the Dale Earnhardt of the Sixties." Without a doubt, he was the one driver fans came to watch the most and the driver every other driver respected and wanted to triumph over.

Fireball was from Palatka, Florida. He won 32 races during a career that lasted from 1950 until May 24, 1964, the day he suffered fatal injuries during a race at Charlotte. Roberts won some big races, such as the 1962 Daytona 500 and Southern 500s in 1958 and 1963. Interestingly enough, Roberts is considered possibly the greatest driver to never win the NASCAR Grand National championship. He was on top of his game when he crawled into his Holman-Moody Ford that terrible day in May, the day he was fatally burned in a crash on the seventh lap of the 1964 World 600.

I was not in attendance at the speedway that day, but I got a phone call with the news. I knew Roberts mostly through interviews and various garage conversations from when I first entered the sport in 1958 until Roberts's death some seven years later. Roberts was 35 years old when he passed away on the morning of July 2, 1964, at Charlotte Memorial Hospital. He had to endure many painful surgeries during the weeks following the crash, and reports circulated that his condition was improving. Even though it was all but certain he would never race again, his doctors hoped for a miraculous recovery. Sadly, that didn't come.

By late June, the infections his doctors feared finally set in. Roberts contracted blood poisoning from the intense burns that covered 70 percent of his body.

I remember the racing fraternity had just arrived at Daytona International Speedway for the running of the Firecracker 400 when word began to spread of Fireball's death. The sport had lost its first superstar, and his loss made the mood in the garage area very heavy. No one wanted to race or wanted to even be at the race track. Everyone's focus definitely wasn't on the job at hand.

Fireball was buried in Daytona Beach on July 5, 1964, at the Bellevue Memorial Park located a couple of miles from the speedway. Over 1,000 people attended his funeral that day, most of them from the racing community. People who have visited his gravesite have noted the sounds of race cars in the distance as they stood and paid their respects to their fallen hero.

Oftentimes, drivers of the Sixties would say they didn't have close friendships with other drivers, considering the fact that one wrong turn of the wheel or one blown tire could result in the unthinkable. But friendships did exist, and Roberts enjoyed a few close ones of his own.

Junior Johnson and Fireball were about as close as any two drivers at any time. They had a great respect for one another. I think to this day that's why Junior quit driving at the end of 1966, two years after Fireball died. Junior was involved in the wreck, along with Ned

Jarrett. The contact with Junior's car sent Fireball into a crossover gate on the backstretch. The wreck wasn't anyone's fault, one way or another. It was just an incident that happened as the field came off turn two. But it affected Junior. From that day forward, he was never the same.

I remember Roberts as he was away from the reporters and away from the camera flashes. Even though he was looked upon as NASCAR's premier driver, he could loosen up his demeanor when away from the pressures and concerns of driving a race car.

Fireball was better known to those outside racing as "Glenn." But he gained the nickname "Fireball" not from driving race cars but from pitching sandlot softball.

Fireball was a really hard man to get to know. Really hard. He loved life. He had a lot of fun. He really enjoyed himself when he wasn't at the race track, because being there meant pressure to win and worries about the car. He was never comfortable around the race tracks, and often you would see him smoking a cigarette when standing around the garage area.

But talk about running wide open. Fireball and Joe Weatherly would wake me up outside my hotel room. They would be drinking, raising the devil and chasing women around the hotel. They really did. They would stay up until daylight drinking and then go and jump in the race car at 12 noon or 1 p.m. and it never seemed to affect them at all. And when Weatherly wasn't partying with Fireball he would be partying with Curtis Turner. I don't know how they could party like they did and still drive 500 miles the next day.

Fireball didn't like doing interviews. I tried once to get him to help with taping some public service radio spots to be played during races. He was rather uncomfortable doing them and would usually decline.

I tried to interview him, and this was in 1961 or '62 and it was really the first time I had interviewed him. I wrote up some public service announcements that I wanted to run at the station. They basically said, "This is Fireball Roberts. Racing is for the race track, not for the highway." And each one went a little bit longer than that.

Some drivers did okay with them. Some tried to do them but mumbled and fumbled through. But I'll bet Fireball tried it 15 times and never could get it. He would miss a word or stumble over something. Finally, he handed the paper back to me and said, "I can't do anything like that. Hell, I'm a damned race car driver. I can't read that." And he turned around and walked off.

Fireball had a unique voice, a deep, resonant speaking voice, but he never liked to talk with any radio people. I don't why, he just didn't.

I enjoyed our brief friendship. I enjoyed seeing a different side of Fireball when he was around friends and away from the public eye. Sadly, he had already been working on plans to retire at the end of the 1964 season and had verbally agreed to work as a spokesperson promoting Falstaff Beer. That opportunity never came.

He and I had a decent relationship, and through Junior, I got to know him pretty well. He didn't like to talk to writers or to anybody else, for that matter. He would always say, "Well, you saw the race and this happened or that happened." He would just brush it off as quickly as he could. I think he was extremely shy, I really do. Even though he could get out and drive a car and win races, he was quiet and introverted, unless you found him out at about two o'clock in the morning with about four snuff glasses full of what Junior used to make. Then he would get pretty vocal.

7

DANGERS AT DAYTONA

I f you've never seen the Daytona International Speedway from the grandstands, I'm here to tell you it's a pretty big place that can generate some pretty fast speeds. I've endured some close calls while being stationed out at the bottom of those high-banked turns, and some of the accidents that have taken place there have been rather scary.

When the place was built, very few of the stock car boys had ever seen anything that big, much less raced on such a big track. Before Daytona, Darlington was the biggest track out there. Daytona was over a mile longer than Darlington, and to some, it was the most intimidating thing around.

When drivers got to Daytona when it opened in '59, some had never turned laps over 150 miles per hour in their entire careers. The cars of the times hadn't turned speeds that fast, either, so it was a whole new untested chapter of NASCAR racing. After extensive practice sessions, the pole position speed for the inaugural Daytona 500 held on February 22, 1959, was 140.121, and it was set by a driver named Bob Welborn.

Speed can be good and bad for anyone working as a turn announcer, including me. I had to be in position to be able to describe the action, which was exciting, but on more than one occasion, I found myself in potential danger while describing those fender-to-fender battles. There were even times when I had to dodge wheels and pieces of race cars when accidents occurred.

Stock cars of the early 1960s very much resembled what you might find in the driveways of homes across the United States. Aside from a few modifications to the body, such as the blocking of headlights and taillights and the installation of roll bars and some beefed-up wheels, they could have been found on any dealership show-room floor.

When parts and pieces flew off of race cars back then, they were real. They were the heavy metal pieces being thrown into the air, not the lighter fiberglass stuff used in new cars today.

The first thing I thought of was how I couldn't believe I was even out there, much less thinking about working. The second thing was the fact that I thought being there was the greatest thing in the world. I know they had well over 60 cars in the field for some of those early Daytona 500 races, including the first. Even after they made a lap or two, I just couldn't believe they could race like that. They were blazing around Daytona at maybe 155 miles per hour. But that seemed like space-shuttle speed to me at the time. It was a heck of a thrill. Only a couple of years later, that pole speed rose to nearly 175 miles per hour (174.910 set by Paul Goldsmith) and was a little hard to believe, too.

Every era of NASCAR racing has had its stars of the day. I remember some of the talented and aggressive drivers of the late 1950s and early 1960s. Back then, it was Lee Petty, Fred Lorenzen, Jack Smith, Ned Jarrett, David Pearson, and Fireball Roberts. They were the guys who ran at the front of the field no matter what happened. They didn't change positions all that much, so you just had to set in your mind to pick up the lead driver and you just kept your eye on him. You could kind of play off of what he and the drivers behind him were doing.

Many of the places where I was positioned weren't the safest pieces of real estate to call races from. The need to be up high enough to see meant improvising at the last minute. I would often be holding a microphone with one hand and holding on for dear life to whatever I was standing on with the other.

The third race I ever worked at Daytona, which was the 1962 Daytona 500, featured one rather frightening moment. Dick Huffman was in charge back then and he put me in turn three at Daytona after starting me in turn four for the '61 Daytona 500 and '61 Firecracker 400 in July. That was many years before MRN came into existence.

The track workers built a very high scaffold, maybe 25 feet in the air, and it was several sections of construction-type scaffolding. They put plywood on top of it for me to stand on, and I had to climb the rounds of scaffolding to get to the plywood. And they had a telephone line that ran up to my position, so if anything happened to that phone line, I was off the air.

This particular Daytona 500 was a wild one. The flagman dropped the green, and Bobby Isaac and Buck Baker were leading this pack of cars when there was a big pile-up. The crash was in turn two, and I was all the way down the backstretch in turn three. They had two cables that tied down the scaffold I was standing on. One cable tied it down in the front, and one in the back kept the wind from rocking it.

Well, Isaac and Baker bounced off of each other two or three times, and both cars kept spinning halfway down the backstretch. As they were doing so, I was describing the action. I was saying, "They're spinning, they're in the grass," etc. Baker was coming and coming and coming, and I could see he was going to hit this poorly constructed, so-called tower I was standing on. There was nothing I could do, because I wasn't going to jump the 25 feet to the ground. I reasoned to myself that that would really hurt.

Baker had bled off most of the speed, but he was still coming at a pretty good clip. I remember he hit the cable in the front of the scaffold, and thank God the thing stopped. The track workers had driven the cable deep into the ground with an iron stob, and the cable anchored to it wasn't but about two or three feet long. When Baker hit that cable, it jerked the tower forward toward the race track, and I thought I was going to be dumped right out onto the racing surface. The cable in the back held it just enough to stop it from going over on the track, but the stob in the back did pull out, and the thing was kind of sitting there rocking, and I was holding on as tightly as I could. I got to thinking after all that was over, "This really ain't the best place to be during a race."

As I said, Huffman was then in charge of the network out of WNBD in Daytona. I told him I just wasn't crazy about getting up there again, and he told me he didn't think that would ever happen again in a race. He said, "That's a heck of a view and it won't happen again." I just told him I didn't want to be that close to the track. They moved me behind a sand bank, thinking if a car got loose and hit the sand bank, it would hit it and slow down before it got to the turn announcer—me. If he hit the sand bank, he probably wouldn't get to me.

It's a pretty helpless feeling when you see a race car speeding for the tower you're sitting on. That wreck with Isaac and Baker really scared the heck out of me.

8

CRAZY CURTIS AND CRAZY JOE

I f there was ever a driver who seemed to live minute to minute and got the most possible out of each one, it was Curtis Turner. Like so many other drivers, his passions in life were racing and flying his airplane. But Turner did both his way, which usually meant wild and unpredictable.

For those who flew with him, it was usually quite an adventure. His untimely death came in an airplane, and 36 years later, many theories remain as to why it went down.

When Curtis flew his airplane, those who flew with him swore they would never do it again. Turner flew just about the way he drove his race cars; wide open and fearless, as if he knew it was the last day he would ever live. He lived his entire life that way, from sun up to sundown.

Believe it or not, Curtis once landed his airplane on a street in Easley, South Carolina, when he spotted the home of a friend he knew. The story goes that he was out of liquor and was sure the friend below had an ample supply. Curtis circled around and lined up with the street the friend lived on, used it as a runway and parked right outside the friend's house. After getting a few fifths for the road, Turner took off. He was doing fine until his wheels caught on some power lines with his tail wheel. The lines snapped and knocked out power to several houses in the area. When he landed in Charlotte, the Federal Aviation Administration guys were there to question him as to what possessed him to land on a public street and to also take his license. He had to know they would be waiting for him.

Turner's closest friend was Joe Weatherly, a NASCAR champion who was killed at the start of the 1964 season on the road course at Riverside, California. The two were as famous for their flying adventures as they were for their all-night partying. Weatherly was known as a clown around the garage area, always pulling pranks on people, always doing something crazy. He would show up in the garage area wearing a pair of pants with one leg blue and the other leg green. Or there would be times he'd wear a brown right shoe and a black left shoe. He was just like Curtis, often living for the minute and having a blast in the process.

Racing folklore seems to always feature stories of Curtis and Joe drinking and carousing until sunrise. Then they would arrive at the race track and take naps on the deck lids of their race cars an hour or two before driving 500-mile races. And many times they would win. I remember Curtis curled up sleeping on the deck lid of the Wood Brothers Ford the morning of the first race at Rockingham, North Carolina in October of 1965. He went on to win that race. It was his first win since being banned four years earlier by France.

And when it came to his race cars, a lot of times Turner drove them with few or no adjustments. He was set to drive a race for the Wood Brothers once back in the early 1960s, and Leonard Wood asked him to get in the car and take a few laps to test the car. Turner smiled and put his right leg through the driver's side window opening, put his foot on the seat and said, "It feels fine to me."

About the time driver suits became mandatory in the early 1960s, Bill France told Turner he had to have a suit next time he drove in a race. France meant a driver's suit, but Turner came to the track wearing a nice suit and tie. He crawled in the car and drove in the race wearing that suit and tie and a helmet. Turner thought that was pretty funny, but I don't think France did.

When he wasn't partying, Curtis was a pretty good businessman and had several businesses during his lifetime, including a large lumber business in Virginia and also had heavy investments in what was then known as Charlotte Motor Speedway. Some say he had gained and lost several fortunes in his lifetime. He could easily sell people on his ideas, and a lot of them were good ones.

I remember listening to people tell stories about flying with him to various places. They also told me they didn't do it but once. Curtis was someone who was wide open all the time, and he did a lot of crazy things in his life, things I guess most people wouldn't do. That included during his airplane flights.

He was on a business trip when he died in a plane crash in Pennsylvania in October of 1970. There were a dozen different theories surrounding why that plane went down, but no one really knows the truth. Some people have said they had the wrong kind of fuel on board. Others said the fuel was contaminated. Others said he had the plane on autopilot and was in the back asleep when one of the engines quit. Nobody really knows for sure.

I do know for a fact that one thing he did, whether he was with someone or by himself, was put the plane on autopilot and take a nap. He had an alarm clock that he used to set when he was close to landing. And Joe Weatherly always carried an alarm clock in his plane and did the same thing. I've talked to a lot of people who have flown with Turner who saw him do it. A lot of people who flew with him had absolutely no flying experience whatsoever, and most of them never flew with him again. He'd tell them to wake him up in 20 minutes or whatever. They thought he was kidding, but he'd go crawl in the back seat and leave them up there shaking in their shoes. It was a pretty frightening experience, but that was just the way Curtis was.

9

"YOU'RE GOIN' TO JAIL!"

n order to broadcast a stock car race, the first rule of thumb is to be able to get into a certain position in order to call the action.

I have experienced my share of roadblocks when trying to get to my designated tower or turn. I've been confronted by track security guards, police officers, and sheriff's deputies.

Of all the race tracks I've been to in my 45 years of racing, I've had the hardest time it seems at Daytona International Speedway. For the life of me, I can't understand it, but it's the place where I've had the most problems just trying to get out to the turn to do my job. In the early years, there seemed to be some obstacle every time I went there.

I worked turn two most of the time. It was one of my favorite places to broadcast from. That was where a lot of the action seemed to take place.

I always had the right sticker on the car. Enoch Staley, who issued credentials in the early days, would always give me a 17C parking pass. It was good for everywhere, even out on the race track. The problem was that not everybody who worked at the race track knew that.

What I would do about 45 minutes before the race would start was pick up the guys who were broadcasting from turns three and four and take them to their respective spots. After letting them out in turn four and then turn three, I would go on down the backstretch, turn right and park in the infield behind a sand bank that was there at the time. I would climb up to my tower and get set to do the broadcast. I was doing that one time, and a Florida Highway Patrolman pulled up behind me on the backstretch.

I saw the lights flashing when he got behind me, but I thought there were maybe some fans fighting in the infield. He pulled up beside me and motioned for me to pull over. I pulled over, and he came to the window.

I said to him, "What do you need?" He shot back, "I need you, dumbass," I said, "What?" The patrolman yelled, "I need for you to follow me outside. There aren't any personal cars supposed to be on this race track."

This is like 20 or 30 minutes before race time, and I explained who I was and showed him my official working credential and 17C parking pass that was good for out there. I also told him what I was going to do, which was to broadcast from my position. He wasn't buying it. He got out of his car and came to my driver's side window and said, "No, you're not. I'm telling you. There aren't any personal cars allowed out here. You follow me out of here! Come with me."

I tried to explain my story again, and he pulled his gun and stuck it in the window. With that move, he said, "Get out of the car. You're under arrest!"

All I could say at that point was say, "OK," and I left my car right there on the race track. We went down back the backstretch and he asked me again who I was and what I was doing there. I told him one more time. He went through the gate at turn four and we started to go out through the tunnel.

I said to him, "I'd like to have your name and badge number, because when this race starts and they call on national radio for me and I'm not there, I'd like to be able to tell them you kept me from doing my job." But that didn't faze him. So we got out on Speedway Boulevard headed for jail, and it was getting real close to race time. He must have started thinking about it, and he pulled to the edge of the road and asked me again who I was. At that point, I was mad as hell. I said, "I'm not telling you again. I've told you five times. You've arrested me, so arrest me!"

He finally got on his radio and called the tower and asked if anyone knew me. The captain of security came on and said, "Yeah, we know Barney Hall and we're looking for him." The patrolman told him he had me under arrest. The security chief hit the roof and said, "He's got the right credentials and stickers. What are you doing? You get him back over here, and I mean right now!"

The patrolman made a U-turn on International Speedway Boulevard right there in front of the track, turned on his lights and siren and floored it, getting me back over to turn two. I got out of the patrol car and I could hear the engines of the race cars firing up on pit road. I started to walk off, and he hollered at me and said, "Hey, Hall. You're a big man around this race track, but I've got your license number. We'll meet again somewhere on that highway out there. I promise you that!" To that I said, "Yeah, I guess we will." But we never did.

I quickly climbed up to my position and scrambled to get my headset on and hooked up and checked the connections. That was a race I came real close to not being a part of, that's for sure.

Come to think of it, I've been arrested at Daytona three or four times and actually made it to the jail for one of them. Like before, I tried to explain, but there was no convincing the law enforcement officers that I was supposed to be in my broadcast position in the turn. They were determined to take me in, I guess.

We were going to broadcast a Paul Revere 250, which was the old night sports car race, and I had a big scaffold they had set up for me right at the start of the road course there at Daytona.

The radio guys I was working with told me the scaffold was literally out on the road course. They said, "When you get ready to go over there, there's a gate, and we'll give you a key to unlock it and climb on up and do your broadcast." I went over and the gate was locked. I climbed over the fence and went on over to the tower. I saw the sheriff's car pull up close to my car outside the fence. They unlocked the gate and came on over.

At that point, the race was going on. I told Ken Squier, who was in the booth, off the air, "I may have some trouble here in a few minutes. I think I've got the deputy sheriff looking for me." They climbed up and started beating on the door of my little makeshift booth and told me to get down. Again, I explained why I was there and showed my credentials and passes, and they said, "You're not broadcasting a night race. You can't even see a night race!" And I guess they were right, because you really couldn't see anything but the headlights of the cars as they came by.

I called Squier again and told him I needed help. But the deputy was saying, "Get down or I'm going to take you in." I told him I was working, but I got cracked with his night stick. So I told Squier that I was done. I said, "Don't come to me to describe any of the action, because I'm not going to be here." I went down and got in the car and went to jail.

A few calls were made on my behalf, and once again they took me back to the race track. But I didn't do any more broadcasting that night. One crack with a nightstick was enough.

10

A COUPLE OF SCARY FLIGHTS

My friendship with David Pearson grew to be pretty strong by the early 1970s. Both of us spent a great deal of time flying together to races across the country, often bypassing the routine commercial airlines in return for the chance to move from place to place faster and easier.

Like me, Pearson enjoyed flying and did so every time the opportunity presented itself. Like so many associated with the sport, the airplane is a great tool for a driver who has a busy schedule of races and many personal appearances.

During one of our many trips, the two of us encountered some bad weather while flying to Daytona Beach for what was then known as the Firecracker 400. This would be one of many anxious flights over the years.

I flew with David for about six or seven years in the same ole' airplane. He had an Aztec built by Piper Aircraft, and it was a pretty good little airplane. We had a lot of fun in that thing, but we also had a few scary moments in it a time or two.

We were flying down there to Daytona, and David had just gotten his instrument rating. Just as we got into the area, the place was socked in for miles. It was really foggy, and the ceiling was probably less than a hundred feet as far as visibility. It was less than an eighth of a mile, which is right at minimums.

We were setting up an approach to the airport, and I was tempted to tell him I thought we should go somewhere else. That was the first time he had ever attempted an instrument approach.

We got set up on course and were coming in to land. We were coming in over Interstate 95 headed toward the beach. The traffic control guys in Daytona were giving us reports at different times from the tower. It was really foggy, almost like taping up the windows of the cockpit with paper. We just couldn't see a thing.

Then a voice unfamiliar to us came over the radio. Both Pearson and I caught our breaths as we looked at one another in disbelief.

Out of nowhere came this voice on the radio that said, "Daytona tower, this is Cessna November 156. I'm trying to get to Jacksonville, and I just thought I'd let you know I'm in your air space following I-95. I'm right down on the deck." It was a student pilot who was lost. That really got my attention!

David looked at me and said, "What do you think?" I told him to stay with it. Finally, we saw the lights of the airport. We were a little bit below minimums at that time. We should have pulled up and come on around. That was one time I was really eating up the seats. They didn't have the student pilot on radar and he couldn't have been 50 feet above the highway. But that was right in our field of flight. That's how midair collisions happen. Obviously, we made it to the ground without hitting him, but it was rather scary there for a few minutes.

There was another trip I was flying that really scared me back in about 1975 or '76. We were going to Michigan International Speedway, and we were flying on top of a really vicious thunderstorm just about the time we got ready to land. We were in touch with Cleveland Air Traffic Center, and Dick Brooks, a longtime race car driver and later a broadcaster with MRN, was with us. I was flying from the right front seat. Sometimes I would work the radio, and sometimes I would fly a little bit, too. I was flying this flight and wishing I wasn't.

Air traffic told us we had to lose eight thousand feet in the next five minutes. That's coming down pretty quickly. I said to David, "We need to check and make sure this weather doesn't make us run into something." But David said, "Oh, they've got us on radar and they know what they're doing."

So we started down and you could see the clouds under us, and they were rolling and really mean looking. When we got into the clouds we could hardly see each other. Thunder and lightning was sounding like dynamite, and it was popping all around the airplane. I looked at the altimeter, which tells you if you're going up or down. It went 900 feet in about two or three seconds. And then it went the other way. We were getting kicked around pretty badly, and I didn't think we were going to come out of that one.

We switched off, and David flew for a while. David was doing all he could to keep the plane straight and level, but he couldn't. I finally looked down and found a hole in the stuff. I recognized the Interstate right at the Holiday Inn where we would stay when we were there for races. Before that, we didn't have a clue where we were. I told David if he would make a right turn and get this thing down real quick, we were only about two or three miles from the airport. So he did, and he really kicked it down.

There was a direct lightning strike right below us, and it looked like the building blew up. Two people were killed in the shelter because of it. We finally landed, but I really thought that was it for us.

Just before we encountered the bad weather, we were having a serious conversation about death and all we had accomplished in our lives. The conversation was quite different once we landed.

The conversation was prompted because there had been a driver who had been seriously injured and almost lost his life the week before. Before the flight, we had been talking about how if this were our last weekend or last day on earth. We talked about how we were way ahead of everybody else, but all of a sudden, I changed my mind. I decided there were a bunch of things I hadn't done yet. Brooks was laughing and said, "I thought you said you were ready to go." I said, "I am ready. Ready to get on the ground and get the hell out of this airplane."

In addition to being one of NASCAR's best drivers ever, David was an excellent pilot. He worked and trained very hard to get his instrument license so he could use his airplane in almost any weather conditions.

When David first started flying back in the mid-1960s, he had a frightening experience at what was then known as Charlotte Motor Speedway. At one time, there was a parking lot just off turns three and four, and a few of the drivers would land there on race morning before it filled up with cars. It could be a great place to take off from if there weren't too many cars in the area. It didn't always work out too well.

Once after a race, David came out to the parking lot to take off to go home to Spartanburg, S.C. As he looked at the line he needed to use to take off, the parking lot was pretty clear except for two or three cars parked in such a way that we couldn't get a straight take-off run.

So he waited about an hour, and when no fans came out to move the cars, he decided he could zigzag between them and get airborne.

As he started his take-off run, there was a fellow who had had too much to drink who was asleep in one of the cars. When he heard the airplane engine and woke up, he opened the car door right into the wing tip on David's plane.

Fortunately, as it turned out, Pearson was able to take off, but it did put a dent in his wing and knocked half the door off and bent what was left all the way back on its hinges. David flew on to Spartanburg and thought he may have hit something but he wasn't sure. The guy who owned the car just happened to be a big fan of David's and a big fan of the Wood Brothers team he drove for. David signed quite a few autographs for the guy, and he was happy as could be. No one was hurt in the deal.

It could have been tragic for David. That was one day that really got his attention in that airplane.

11

BUSTED

Many terms have been coined over the years to describe racing, giving various descriptions a vocabulary that only race fans understand.

For instance, over the years, race engines have been "blown, blowed, lost, hand-grenaded, dropped" and even "exploded." But during a superspeedway race in the early 1970s, the word "busted" was possibly defined for its truest meaning.

We were on the air during a race at Daytona, and I remember one particular unexpected conversation between the broadcast booth and pit road that went out to radio stations across the nation.

When Ken Squier first came from up north to anchor Motor Racing Network in 1972, we were at Daytona International Speedway and I was working one of the turns. One of the guys helping us that day was Chris Economaki, a longtime radio and television announcer who worked with both ABC Sports and CBS Sports covering NASCAR races. This particular day, he was working the garage and pit road for us in the early days of MRN radio.

There was a caution and Squier said on the radio that someone had blown an engine and had pulled into the garage area. Ken went on to talk about how the driver had lost the engine and was dropping oil and smoking and had gone behind the wall with a busted motor.

Squier finally said, "Let's go down to Chris Economaki on pit road for the story."

Chris's high voice came on the air, and if you remember Chris, he didn't usually hold very much back. He said, "Squier, your use of the English language is atrocious. There is no such thing as a 'busted' motor. He may have a blown-up motor, or something to that effect, but he certainly doesn't have a busted motor." Chris went on to say, "Now, Linda Vaughn, Miss Unocal, on the other hand, who is standing right here with me, is busted!"

There was dead silence for a few seconds and everyone fumbled around and recovered and got back to the race. I heard the comment and had to regain my composure before I could talk. I was laughing my tail off over there in the turn.

You just never ever knew what Chris Economaki was going to say.

12

BANJO AND HIS RENTAL CAR

Among race car drivers, rental cars seem to be too much of a temptation, especially if they are shiny and have a few extra horses under their hoods. Countless fenders, doors, and bumpers have been replaced over the past 56 years of NASCAR racing. At times, rental cars have been pulled from motel swimming pools, cornfields, and a vacant parking lot or two after "somehow" ending up there.

I know of two stories involving the late Edwin Keith "Banjo" Matthews and rental cars, but there are probably many more. They occurred sometime in the mid-1970s.

First, a little history about Banjo is in order. Banjo was born in 1932 and won hundreds of modified races as a driver, starting when he was about 15 years old. He drove in 50 NASCAR Grand National races but had more success as a team owner. His cars started 160 races from 1963 through 1971 and won 14 pole positions and nine races with various drivers. Fireball Roberts, A.J. Foyt, and Donnie Allison all won races at Daytona in his cars, with Allison also winning for Banjo at Charlotte and Rockingham. Junior Johnson won races in his cars as well. Banjo probably built a thousand chassis and race cars for other drivers and teams over the years.

Sadly, we lost Banjo on October 2, 1996. He had been in declining health for about 10 years and had been very sick for about two years before his death.

Banjo was a character, and we had a lot of fun with him. David Pearson used to hide Banjo's keys a lot. We would ride with Banjo from the hotel to the race tracks, especially when there were races at Charlotte. But because of Pearson, Banjo was always looking for his keys.

Banjo would on occasion bend his elbow a little more than he should have at the bar the night before and wouldn't remember some things, specifically where his car keys were. Well, David would take his keys a lot to play a trick but also so he wouldn't lose them. But one morning David said he was going to tell him he didn't have his keys. As it turned out, he really didn't have his keys, because he forgot and left them in the ignition. When they went outside to get in the car to go to the track, someone really had stolen the car. But Banjo was like, "Come on, David. This isn't funny. Where's my car?" And David said, "Banjo, I really don't know. Somebody got it!" I think until the day he died, Banjo thought David had taken the car that day and hidden it somewhere.

The other time Banjo had a problem with a rental car was when they, or I should say we, used to race from the Darlington raceway track back to the old Sheraton Hotel in Darlington. There were about 10 miles of back roads there in the country around the track, and all the guys who had rental cars would end up on that road at the same time. We were always passing one another and bumping one another to see who could get back to the hotel first.

Banjo and David and Bobby Allison were all racing back to the hotel one day, and Banjo got bumped by Pearson. He lost control and went flying out through a soybean field and hit a pretty good-sized pecan tree right out in the middle of it. I was riding with Pearson, and we all stopped and went back to check on Banjo. It didn't hurt him, but it really caved in the front of his car. We left the car right there in the field and took Banjo back to the hotel so he could use the phone in David's room to call the rental car company. He called over to the Florence, South Carolina office and tried to explain the situation to the rental agent as best he could.

Banjo said, "Hey, this is Banjo Matthews, and I'm going to need another rental car." The agent said, "Well, what's wrong with the one you have?"

Banjo said, "Well, it won't run." The guy in the rental car office asked, "Well, why won't it run?" Banjo thought for a second and said, "The motor in it won't run." The agent said, "Do you have any idea why?" Banjo finally came clean and said, "Well, basically because the motor is stuck all the way back to the front seat." He went on to explain his way out of it, blaming it on a dog that ran out in front of him or something like that.

The motor in Banjo's rental car really was through the firewall and embedded into the front seat. It's a wonder it didn't kill him when he hit that tree.

13

AMBULANCES IN THE AREA

In the excitement of the moment, innocent mistakes can happen on the air. During an event at Talladega Superspeedway (then known as Alabama International Motor Speedway) on May 6, 1973, a word was presented to me over the airwaves that I simply wasn't familiar with. Obviously, there wasn't time to find a dictionary, especially having been positioned out in the turn. So I had to go with my gut feeling. Unfortunately, that gut feeling was wrong.

I laugh about it now, but the story I'm about to tell you wasn't very funny at the time. There was a huge wreck at Talladega that seemed to happen in waves. There were 60 cars in the field that day, and when they wrecked, some of them were on their roofs and others had taken some hard crashes. Some of the drivers in the field had never driven that fast and didn't really have the racing experience to be out there. Thick smoke developed on the backstretch, and those running behind the main wreck didn't slow down. When the main cause of the crash finally stopped, a second and third group of cars came plowing in. It was like the wreck that wouldn't stop happening. Unfortunately,

Hall handles the prerace announcing duties at the Alabama International Motor Speedway in the mid-1970s. The 2.66-mile track is now known as the Talladega Superspeedway. *Motorsports Images & Archives. Used with permission.*

Wendell Scott and several others suffered serious injuries as a result of that crash.

Well, I was never that great in school, especially in English. I guess on that day I sort of proved that.

Ken Squier came to me on the radio to pass it off for a description of what had happened in front of me. Ken said, "That was a really bad wreck down there. Let's go to Barney Hall for an update. Barney, are any of those guys ambulatory?"

If you really want to know the truth, I didn't even know what the word ambulatory meant. Before that day, I had never even heard the word. I said, "Yeah, Ken, there are several of them being picked up by ambulances and will be taken to the infield care center. There are plenty of ambulances here on the scene right now."

There was dead silence on the network for half a minute. I still didn't know what I had done, I really didn't. Squier finally came back and said, "Uhhh, okay, Barney."

When I got back to the meeting after the race, Squier said, "Do you known what you said up there?" I honestly had no idea and said, "No, what?" Ken said, "Do you know what ambulatory means?" I said, "I thought it meant they were in the ambulance and they were going to take them to the hospital."

Everybody just laughed and shook their heads. I had no idea it meant they were able to walk around on their own power. I honestly didn't.

For several years, somebody would come up to me and ask me if there were any ambulances in the area. I heard that comment for quite some time.

14

COKE OR PEPSI?

For me, there has been more than one embarrassing moment during 45 years of broadcasting. One, however, came closer than any other as the one that nearly cost me my career.

This particular day in February of 1968, I was working in the pits for a USAC event at the Daytona International Speedway. I learned firsthand that getting the sponsor's name right was one of the most important jobs a race announcer has.

I've made my fair share of mistakes on the air, but that day at Daytona had to be the all-time worst. It came very close to costing me my job.

The story centered on Jim Hurtubise, a USAC driver in both open-wheel and stock cars. He also ran a few seasons of limited schedules in NASCAR competition. Hurtubise suffered a terrible Indy Car crash at Milwaukee in 1964 and sustained burns over 40 percent of his body. He insisted that his doctors permanently position his badly burned hands in such a way that he could grip a race car steering wheel. Jim died of a heart attack on January 6, 1989.

Hurtubise had gotten a nice sponsorship deal from Pepsi Cola for some USAC stock car events in 1968. Daytona was a big race on their schedule because the soft drink was quite prominent in all the machines and vending areas around the track and still is today.

This particular afternoon, Joan Crawford, the movie actress, was in attendance as a special guest of Bill France, Sr. She was the longtime chairman of the board of the Pepsi Cola Co., having been appointed to the position after her husband, Alfred Steele, died of a heart attack on April 19, 1959.

Hurtubise had a problem with his No. 56 Mercury in the early laps of the race and continued to come down pit road. I noticed he had been coming in quite a bit more than usual.

He must have made 25 pit stops the first 50 laps of the race. In fact, it seemed like he was coming in almost every lap. He was pitting down pit road and from where I was tied to a telephone line that I couldn't leave. I had a pit runner with me that day who was helping get information for me. I asked him to go up and find out why Hurtubise was making so many stops. Ken Squier was in the booth and he called down and asked me to check on what was going on and I told him we were doing just that.

In the meantime, Buddy Baker was leading the race and had a problem and had to make an unscheduled pit stop. So I ran over there and tried to stand up on the wall so I could see what Baker's crew was going to do to his car. All I could see was they were working under the hood of Baker's car and I was saying what they were doing on the radio. In the meantime, this kid who was running for me came back, and the information he usually passed on was written on a big card for me to read since the engines were so loud. He had written the words, "He has stopped for a sandwich and a Coke!" The guys on the crew recognized he was a young kid who was new to the game and were pulling his leg with the "Coke" remark. He really thought they were serious.

I was talking about Baker and was quite concerned with what was going on with him. The pit runner poked me and I turned around in the heat of the moment. He showed me what was written on the sign and I was struggling to find something to say about Baker. So I said on the air, "By the way, Ken, the reason Hurtubise is pitting so much is because he's grabbing a sandwich and a Coke."

The minute I said that you could have hit me with a sledgehammer because I knew I had said the wrong thing about as quickly as I said it. In my mind, I was thinking, "Oh my God, what have I just said?" It scared me so bad I just shut up for the rest of the afternoon. I figured right then and there they are going to fire my butt! Maybe even right there on the spot.

So the race was almost over, and the producer, Roger Bahre, called me from the tower. He said, "Barney, you need to come to the tower as soon as this race is over." I said I would. I was sure I was just going up there to get fired. I knew Bill France, Sr. was up there. I thought my days as a broadcaster were over.

I walked in and Roger marched me over to Bill Sr. who was standing at the other side of the room. Standing close by him was Joan Crawford, and I could tell she wasn't happy.

"This is Barney Hall, the pit announcer you wanted to see," Roger announced to Ms. Crawford in an apologetic tone. Crawford walked over to me and gazed at me hard for a moment.

Ms. Crawford said, "I didn't think your comment was too cute. That's not the way to be funny." Before I could speak, Bill Sr. piped in and asked, "Mrs. Crawford, what do you think we should do about this situation?"

She thought for a moment and said, "Make sure it doesn't happen again." With that she turned and began to leave the room. "I'll take care of it," Bill Sr. assured her.

I admit I was shaking a bit after the awkward confrontation. I asked Roger if I was fired and he said he couldn't tell me. Bill Sr. came over after Ms. Crawford left and said, "Boy, what in the world were you thinking?" I said, "Sir, I don't know. If you fire me, I don't blame you." I really meant that.

I've thought about that day many times during my career and I've often wondered why I wasn't fired. The fact is my comment came across as a joke and that may have been my only saving grace. I just simply put my brain out of gear and said that. That's probably the only thing that helped me keep my job.

Part of the problem was that Squier, who was the lead announcer, demanded that we never have dead air or time on the radio where nothing is said. Right or wrong, say something. That day I said the wrong thing and wish I could have taken it back. I'll promise you this; it's something that I've been ribbed about for a lot of years.

15

MY FRIEND DAVID PEARSON

hadn't looked to build a friendship with NASCAR driver David Pearson, but circumstances simply dictated it. In 1974 we were both standing in a hotel lobby looking for a steak or seafood and neither wanted to eat alone.

What occurred over that meal was the beginning of a friendship that has lasted for over 30 years.

As I was standing in the lobby of the hotel, Pearson said, "Are you gonna go eat?" I said, "Yeah, I'm alone." He invited me to go with him, so I did. That was back in the days when it was pretty common for a driver to invite a media member out to dinner because they simply weren't as busy and being pulled in all directions like they are today.

We went to dinner and just got to talking about different things. I had an inside track and I knew a little bit more of what was going on in NASCAR than the average bear did, I guess. We'd talk about different stuff.

I remember how Pearson and I seemed to hit it off so easily, due to the fact that we are both quiet, and soft spoken and we found we shared many of the same interests. I also think the friendship began because of something much deeper.

I guess Pearson and I became friends because I was honest with him. Back then, David was the superstar, and everyone said what they thought David wanted to hear. At that particular time in the mid-1970s, he was winning a lot of races with Holman-Moody and later with the Wood Brothers.

His first race with the Wood Brothers was April 16, 1972, at Darlington Raceway in what was then known as the Rebel 400. I was at that race but wasn't broadcasting it. I remember how special that day was because Pearson crawled in the car and won with it right off the bat. It was also special because a lot of people thought he was over the hill and was too old to win. A lot of people were saying the Wood Brothers should have put A.J. Foyt or Cale Yarborough in the car, but David obviously wasn't over the hill at all. Boy, those who said he couldn't win anymore were wrong.

Pearson went on to win a lot of races for the Woods over the next seven or eight years. In 1973, they only entered 16 superspeedway races, but he won 11 of them. That's how good they were together. I can't think of a more successful hook-up between a driver and team owner than David and the Wood Brothers. He was truly one of the best.

David used to say he didn't like to practice the car. He would say, "Just fix it the way you think it should be, and I'll drive it." Leonard Wood, his crew chief during all their success together, would shoot back, "Well, David, you may not need the practice, but the car sure does."

Another funny story involved David and his team owner, Glen Wood. One day, David was getting ready to go out and qualify and he looked over to Glen and said, "Hey, give me my hemet!" Glen looked at him and said, "Give you what?" David said, "My hemet! Give me my hemet!" Glen finally figured out he meant his helmet. Part of that was his South Carolina accent.

Throughout his career, David was rather quiet and didn't talk much and still doesn't talk much today. But he could sure get the job done in a race car.

If David had had the outgoing personality that Richard Petty did to mingle with the fans and was comfortable doing it, he would have been even more popular than he was. NASCAR or sponsors would have different things that David would need to go to, such as nightly functions after being at the track all day. But David just wouldn't go. He didn't like to go to a lot of that stuff.

During the times they would have the dinners honoring the defending winner at Talladega, it was a big deal from the City of Birmingham, but David didn't like going to them. I remember once there was a banquet at which David was being honored for winning at Talladega. I didn't know about the dinner being in David's honor, so we went and played tennis together that night, and the newspapers just crucified him the next day for not showing up. I got on Pearson's case really bad about it during the flight home together that weekend. I tried to explain to him and Bobby Isaac how important it was.

Come to think of it, Isaac never did go to functions like that, either. He wouldn't go to anything that he could get out of.

I finally got David to go to some press parties as they called them back then. He had fun once he started coming out of his shell. David has a great sense of humor. He was great with fans as well. Now you can't get him to shut up! He's my friend, so I'm razzing him there a little. David is just a shy person and always has been. But he's a really great guy.

16

THE GREAT BOBBY ALLISON

O ne driver absolutely determined to make it as a NASCAR driver was Bobby Allison, originally from Miami, Florida, but he made his home during his driving career in Hueytown, Alabama.

From 1960 until 1988, Allison won a total of 84 races, even though one victory he collected fair and square at Bowman Gray Stadium never made it into the win column.

That infamous day in 1971, Bill France Sr. realized he would not have a full field of what was then known as NASCAR Grand National cars, and so he allowed the Grand American machines to enter the race. But once the checkered flag dropped and Allison had won, the win was disallowed because he was driving a Grand American car.

For the past 35 years, the win has hung in limbo but should place Allison solidly as the third winningest driver with 85 victories behind Richard Petty with 200 and David Pearson with 105. Presently, Allison sits tied for third with Darrell Waltrip with 84.

After several second-place finishes in the championship battles, including back-to-back runner-up finishes in 1981 and 1982, Allison did finally secure the elusive title in 1983 while driving for Digard Racing Co. and former team owner Bill Gardner. Other team owners he was successful with included Holman and Moody, Junior Johnson, Roger Penske, Bud Moore, Harry Ranier, and Bill and Mickey Stavola.

On June 19, 1988, Allison was involved in a near-fatal accident at Pocono, when his car was hit in the driver's side door, ending his career. After a lengthy recovery period, Allison returned to the race track, both as a spectator as well as a co-team owner, but never again as a NASCAR driver.

I met Bobby Allison about 1963 or 1964, a year or two after they had built what was then known as Bristol International Speedway. Bobby and his brother Donnie came up there, and he wasn't running what was called Grand National back then. I remember him bringing an old modified car up there. He and Donnie beat and banged on each other like you wouldn't believe. I didn't know they were brothers, and when I found out I couldn't believe they were hammering on each other like they did that day.

Like me, Bobby was obsessed with flying airplanes. He's the only man I've ever seen take off in a twin-engine airplane with one engine totally shut down. And he's the only person I know who ever had as severe a head injury as he did (from the Pocono crash) to get his pilot's license back. That was a huge accomplishment for him, or for anyone, for that matter.

Bobby had his plane at Winston-Salem, North Carolina, after a race there and flew it back to Hueytown, Alabama, because it was going to cost him so much money to get it fixed in Winston-Salem. Being a pilot myself, I know what that entails. Still, I wouldn't even attempt to take off with one engine gone like he did. That tells me just how good a pilot he really was. He would have made a great airline pilot.

Bobby and I were flying together to Atlanta once with David Pearson, and Bobby was trying to talk David into buying an Aerostar. Bobby was flying and David was sitting in the right seat. He asked

David, "Ever done a snap roll in your Aztec?" David said, "Hell, no! Are you crazy?"

"Boy, this thing will snap roll real easy," David said. "Let me see." But David was just kidding.

I was just sitting there about to take a swallow of coffee, when all of a sudden, there we went. Somehow, I never spilled a drop of coffee. That's how smooth Bobby was in that airplane. I absolutely couldn't believe I didn't spill a drop. Bobby actually did another snap roll before we landed.

The bad news was there was an FAA inspector giving a student a check ride at Bear Creek Airport close to the track, and he saw Bobby doing those snap rolls. We didn't think anything about the stunt flying he was doing, and when we landed we just got in the car and drove to the race track.

The FAA inspector asked someone at the airport who owned that Aerostar, but the man wouldn't tell him, because he knew the story. The inspector went to the plane and got the identification number from it and found out it belonged to Robert Arthur Allison.

The next day the FAA inspector came to the back gate of the Atlanta race track and wanted to come into the garage to talk with Bobby. Bill Gazaway, who was the NASCAR technical chief at the time, told him he couldn't come in. The FAA inspector told Gazaway he had a citation for whoever was flying that Aerostar.

Gazaway told Bobby he'd better go out to the gate, so Bobby did, and he told the guy he had just left it parked and didn't know who was flying it.

The FAA inspector said, "I'll tell you what. We're going to put a lock on the door and ground it until we figure out who was flying it. It might take a week or it might take a year, but we'll find him. It will sit right there until I find out."

When he said that, Bobby said, "I was the one who did it." It ended it up that Bobby just got a warning, but he could have lost his license and gotten a fine.

Bobby really made his presence known in Winston-Salem in 1965 when he went up against Curtis Turner in a race there at Bowman Gray Stadium. It's an old football field, but they've raced stock cars there for years and still do.

That day Bobby had an old Chevelle he built himself, and he entered it in a NASCAR Grand National race. He kicked everybody's hind end that day. He did that a time or two with that old Chevelle.

Back then, drivers had pretty strong feelings about an outsider coming into the sport, especially as bad as Bobby beat some of the guys in that era. He wasn't supposed to beat all of the big names in that little Chevelle, but he did.

That day at Winston-Salem, he and Turner put on a show; chasing each other down and ramming the hell out of each other. Bobby stood his ground, and so did Curtis. By the end of the night, both of their cars were sitting stalled in the infield with steam everywhere. The fans loved it, and at that point, a lot of them began pulling for Bobby because he wasn't afraid to mix it up with the big-name guys. He was the little man's hero.

Every chance Bobby got, he took a jab at NASCAR. If NASCAR did something he thought was wrong, he would talk to anybody who would write about it in the newspaper or put it on the radio. Of course, that irritated NASCAR. That relationship was never great, at least for the first 20 years he was in this business. I don't think Bobby got the respect he deserved because he was always all over NASCAR's case about something.

You could ask Bobby how his mother was doing, and he would figure out some way to take a jab at NASCAR before the end of the conversation.

I remember one rather awkward interview I had with Bobby that really wasn't an interview.

We had a gentleman in the business a few years back that Bobby worked and drove for, and the relationship wasn't real good, even though they won 10 or 11 races together.

The gentleman he drove for died, and I went to Bobby to get his comment for a piece I was doing for Motor Racing Network. I said, "Bobby, how do you feel about this man that you drove for and his terrible passing?" Bobby simply said, "Well, I'll tell you one thing. If anybody died and went straight to hell, he did!"

I didn't know if he was kidding or what. He turned around and walked off, and I yelled, "Bobby!"

He turned around and said, "What?"

I said, "I can't use that!"

Bobby said, "Well, I'm sorry. That's the way I feel."

He never did come back to say anything flattering about the man. I walked around stunned for half a day. I couldn't believe that. And I don't know to this day, 25 years later, if he was kidding or not. Somehow I don't think he was.

Oftentimes between NASCAR Cup events, drivers would find local short tracks and draw crowds simply by showing up to race. Promoters would pay them to come, and the grandstands would usually fill up.

Some of the best racing I ever saw Bobby do wasn't in NASCAR or in the old Grand National cars, but rather in local short track cars. He and David Pearson used to take deals on weekend tracks. There was a track where they raced down in Georgia, and Pearson and Bobby were both getting an appearance fee to come down and run a Saturday night race. It didn't mean all that much if they won or lost, because that appearance fee was all they were going to get up front for showing up.

They were running first and second, and Pearson was leading this particular night. They had hammered on each other pretty good with Bobby doing most of the hammering. The last lap, they came off turn four and were looking at the checkered flag. Bobby pulled up and turned Pearson right into the wall and tore his old car up pretty badly. Of course, they were in cars that belonged to local drivers. That was about the only time I had ever seen Pearson really get fighting mad at Bobby.

We were flying back on Pearson's plane to the NASCAR race held the next day. They didn't say a whole lot to each other on the way back. They had a great respect for each other, they really did. But that night, it was probably best they didn't talk after what had happened.

David won a lot of races just like Bobby did, and neither one was shy about putting a bumper to the guy in front of him. Bobby would do it in a heartbeat. That was part of the business back in those days. No one would do anything to hurt anyone, but if you knocked someone sideways with 10 laps to go to win the race, it was just an accepted thing.

Bobby and Richard Petty were crossways with each other for 25 years. They probably respected each other, but if one touched the other on the race track, one of the two would go off the deep end.

The race at North Wilkesboro in 1972 sticks out in my mind as a good example of that. Bobby and Richard beat the living fire out of each other the last half of the race. Lap after lap, one would tag the other. The fans really got into it pretty good that day. When we went to victory lane, there was a chicken-wire fence around it to keep the spectators out. Back then you could walk right up to victory lane without a lot of hassle from track security.

They were yelling at Richard because they were in Junior Johnson country, so to speak, and that's who Bobby was driving for. They were yelling, "You S.O.B! We'll get you when you come out (of victory lane)." Half of them were upset with Bobby for giving Richard such a hard time.

I shortened the interview and I got out of victory lane because I didn't know what was going to happen. I remember that race well, and the next two or three times Richard and Bobby came up there, that was what everybody in Wilkes County was talking about. That packed the fans in there at North Wilkesboro for a lot of years.

17

PEARSON AND ISAAC

There are some rather intense rivalries that exist among drivers on the race track, but the feelings can be just the opposite for some drivers when away from the intense fender-to-fender battles.

One very special friendship developed between David Pearson and Bobby Isaac, having started under some rather rocky conditions.

Both David and Bobby enjoyed top rides that helped propel them to NASCAR Grand National championships. Pearson won his titles in 1966 while with team owner Cotton Owens and in '68 and '69 for Ford's Holman-Moody operation and principals John Holman and Ralph Moody. Isaac scored his lone championship in 1970 while with team owner Nord Krauskopf.

They often played tricks on one another, and I was there to watch many of those tricks unfold.

Funny thing is, David and Bobby started out not being very good friends. Back in Bristol during the first or second race ever run there in '62, I was doing P.A. work. Practice lasted all day long, and you could just go out and run about anytime you wanted to. When someone got ready to qualify, they would go and tell John Bruner, then the NASCAR starter, that they were ready to go. NASCAR officials would wave everybody in off the track, and the driver would make a qualifying attempt. Then, after the time was posted, they would open the track up for practice again if no one else wanted to qualify. It could make for a rather long day for those of us who had to stick around the track and announce what was going on.

People who've attended races at the Bristol Motor Speedway in recent years may not realize how much the track has changed. It has evolved into the beautiful showplace that it is today. The track once only had about 25,000 seats and was quite a bit different in its early days of operation. Today there are probably 10 times the seats that were there then.

Bristol's infield was about half-swamp the first few years that thing ran. Pearson had qualified earlier in the day when the track was cool and had a pretty good time. A lot of people thought he would get the pole.

Bobby was getting ready to qualify, and a cloud had come over the track. Even back then, when a cloud came over, it was a good time to qualify because the track would be cooler and you'd turn in a better speed. That really hasn't changed, because that's how it is today. Cooler means faster on most asphalt tracks.

David knew he was going to get beat when Bobby went out. Well, over in turn three and four, there were bushes growing up right at the edge of the track. People find it hard to believe, but there were bushes growing around the track, the kind that grow in swamps or wetlands. They were about head high, and there were about 15 or 20 clumped over there where Pearson was.

When Isaac rolled down pit road and was ready to go out, Pearson went over and hid in those bushes. When Isaac took the green flag and got through turns one and two and headed down the backstretch, Pearson started swinging his arms back and forth trying to spook him or tell him to slow down. Well, Bobby lifted and messed up his run. He slowly made his way back into the pits. He asked NASCAR what the problem was and they said, "There is no problem. What are you talking about?" Isaac said, "Somebody came on the track and motioned for me to slow down, and I need to run again. That's not right!" The NASCAR official he was talking to said, "Well, it wasn't any of us, and the time stands."

Isaac was madder than a wet hen, running all around trying to find out who did it. David was hiding and was afraid Isaac was going to find out it was him. They had a little pushing match after that, but they eventually became pretty good friends. That incident at Bristol sort of broke the ice and got them talking to one another.

I also recall a time when David got the best of Bobby at a traffic light. The two laughed about it for years after.

David and Bobby were at a stoplight, and I was riding with them when we were racing in Bristol after a race in 1963. Bobby was driving for a team who ran Dodges at that time, and he had been given a loaner car from Dodge to drive for the weekend.

So we pulled up to a traffic light, and it was a four-lane highway we were on. We were on the outside lane, and there was a guy on the inside lane in a pick-up truck sitting beside us. Pearson was always playing jokes on Isaac. David said to Bobby, "Don't look out the window, but that guy in that pick-up truck recognizes you and knows we are race car drivers. When that light changes, he is going to try and outdrag you to the next intersection. Don't you let him do it."

Bobby started to look at the guy and David said, "Don't look! Don't look!" The car we were in had one of those floor shift deals. David meant to knock the car in neutral, hoping that Isaac would push the throttle down so we wouldn't go anywhere. Instead, David knocked it in reverse by accident. The car went backward and slammed into the truck behind us. Thank goodness it was a pretty good-sized truck behind us with a big bumper. It tore the rear end of that Dodge up big time. The guy in the truck was going to get out and clean house with all three of us. Fortunately, they were able to smooth things over with an autograph or two. That's just how those two characters were.

Bobby struggled with one issue that was very personal to him throughout his career. He had an immense amount of talent at hustling a race car around a race track. Because of that talent, he got the good rides, which put him in a variety of social circles. But at times, that proved to be a real problem for him. Bobby didn't have a good education and it really bothered him a lot. When he married his wife, Patsy, she helped him learn how to read. I saw him sign some autographs once and people asked him to sign autographs to John or Bob or Bill or whomever. And he would struggle with that. Sometimes there would be names he just didn't know how to spell. So he would often just sign his name and let it go at that.

One event in Bobby's life cost him some good rides in the mid-1970s.

During a race at Talladega in 1973, Bobby was driving for Bud Moore and leading the race by a pretty good margin when he came down pit road, parked the car and crawled out. Bud was furious and asked him why he had parked the car. Bobby said, "I heard voices that told me to."

Of course, Bud didn't like that since he was the car owner and wanted Bobby to get out there and win or at least get a good finish. As usual, I remember Pearson kind of laughed about it. He said probably the only voice he heard was Bud yelling at him in the two-way radio to get that car up there and lead the race. It kind of surprised me, knowing Bobby as well as I did. He would have been the last man in the world I would have thought would climb out of a race car and say, "I heard a voice that told me not to do this. Get out of the car." It shocked a lot of people, including me.

Bobby was going through some personal problems at the time and wasn't winning as many races as he knew he was capable of winning. I think what was going on off the track had a lot to do with what happened that day at Talladega. The bad thing was, he never was able to land any top-flight, full-time rides ever again.

We lost Bobby to a heart attack in August of 1977 at Hickory Motor Speedway. He raced in a Late Model Sportsman event there and began to feel bad immediately afterward. By the time they got him to the hospital, he was gone. Bobby was a real good friend to me, and we had a lot of great times together.

18

PIGGY PACKAGE

There are times when firing up the airplane is of the utmost importance. Some things simply take priority over others. I remember a time when David Pearson had to make an incredibly important trip to a friend's house to pick up a couple of special packages.

Pearson was one of the true characters I've traveled an awful lot with over the years. When David bought a farm around Spartanburg, South Carolina, at the height of his career, he wanted to put some livestock there to raise when he wasn't racing. One of the things he wanted was pigs, and no one ever knew why. That was just a thing with him, I guess. A farm has to have pigs.

I just happened to be visiting with him one day, and he told me we had to make a real important trip. We took his airplane and flew it up to Rockingham, North Carolina, and picked up a couple of pigs from Jane Hogan's friend. Jane is someone who has been around the sport who has had several roles and is truly respected in the business. She is a great cook and has hosted a lot of hospitality functions, including taking care of feeding the media, which has been a nice treat over the years.

Well, Jane's friend raised a lot of pigs and sold them for pork processing. We got there, picked out the two pigs David wanted, and we were soon on our way. Problem was we didn't have anything to put them in, so he put them in a pasteboard box we found empty there at the lady's house.

These pigs were six or eight weeks old and were a pretty good size. We got back to the plane and I told David, "They're going to get out of that box and get all over the airplane." But we put them in there and we took off. We weren't in the air 15 minutes and one had chewed a hole in the side of the box and was running around the airplane. One was back there trying to chew up the upholstery and the carpet and trying to eat anything he could find. Before long, the second one had gotten out, and we had all kinds of, let's say stuff, in the airplane and in the carpet.

David finally looked over at me and asked me to take the controls. I was trying to fly while David was back there getting them back in the box and cleaning up some of the mess.

We finally got back to Spartanburg where David lives and got the pigs settled in their pens. I found out a couple of weeks later that David named the ugly one "Barney" and the pretty one "Jane Hogan."

David was, and still is, quite a character.

19

DAVID MEETS PETER

I t wasn't seen very often, but David Pearson could display a temper when another driver would occasionally make contact with him and cause damage to his car. That holds true with any driver.

I remember one particular incident that occurred at Michigan International Speedway in the early 1970s that gave the fans in attendance a pretty good chuckle.

The first International Race of Champions they ever ran at Michigan involved running Porsche cars. They had a huge mixture of drivers in that thing from every racing sanction you could imagine. A lot of them had never run a high-banked race track before. One of the drivers in the race that day was Emerson Fittipaldi who was running Formula One races at the time.

The guy in the flag stand dropped the green flag, and all these drivers got up to speed. The race got going pretty well, and David was leading. He had to shift gears in the car and really wasn't used to the close gears in the Porsche transmission. He messed up a gear and with that problem solved, he got back in the pack and was trying to work his way back up to the front. When he caught Fittipaldi, he pulled down and they somehow collided, and David wrecked. He had enough damage to his car to put him out. He came back into the garage and got out of his car just fuming.

I wasn't doing the radio broadcast for that race, but I was doing the public address announcing. Chris Economaki and I were working together and he said, "Well, you know David pretty well, so you go talk to him." I walked over to him and asked him what happened. Pearson said, "Well, I'll tell you what happened. That foreign driver ran into me out there. You know who I'm talking about. That guy named Emerson Peterpaldi!"

I just about broke up. You could hear the crowd laughing up in the stands. They got a pretty good chuckle out of it, and I still laugh about that today.

20

FEARLESS FREDDIE

n the early days of NASCAR racing, many of the drivers spent more time turning practice laps and working on their race cars than they did polishing their skills in front of a television camera or giving interviews into a microphone.

There were a select few, though, who worked just as hard at giving good interviews as they did fighting for position on the race track.

Fred Lorenzen, driver of the No. 28 Holman-Moody Ford, was one of them. He was smart, articulate, good looking, and a great asset for promoting NASCAR racing. He was different from the typical grease-covered stereotyped racer in NASCAR's fledgling early days.

Earning the nicknames "Fearless Freddie" and "Golden Boy," Lorenzen established himself as one of the stars of the 1960s, winning 26 races between 1961 and 1966. He was a tough race car driver, always a threat to win, no matter if on a short track or a superspeedway. He routinely mixed it up with the roughest of drivers and never backed down.

In 1963, Lorenzen was the first driver to win $100,000 in a season, claiming $113,570 that year.

In late 1966, Lorenzen announced his retirement from driving, feeling he had won enough money to step away. It was a decision he regrets today, believing he should have stayed in the prominent Holman-Moody ride he had. Most historians feel he would have won more races and might have won a championship.

After his retirement, Lorenzen worked as a team manager for Holman-Moody, offering assistance to Bobby Allison when he joined the operation in 1967. Lorenzen wasn't happy on the sidelines and returned to driving in 1970, but only for limited schedules over the next few years. He was never able to land another top full-time ride and retired for good at the end of the 1972 season.

Even though he made a personal fortune selling real estate around his Elmhurst, Illinois home, his heart has always been in NASCAR.

There were a few drivers who could give good interviews back then, and Fred Lorenzen was one of them. Fred was very polished, and he was probably the best on the air we had. He took a lot of pride in making a good appearance with clean uniforms and also took pride in coming across well.

Fred liked to talk. There wasn't that much television around back then, but there were quite a few radio guys. Fred was very articulate and would listen to what you were asking and give you a good answer to the question and give you decent information.

He was a hard-working boy. The first time I ever saw Fred was at Martinsville about 1961. He seemed to always have his head under the hood of a race car. And he was the first to bring a briefcase to a race track. He would win and then find a pay phone in the garage and call his stockbroker. That was strange to see among a bunch of drivers and mechanics who had no interests other than race cars.

Joe Weatherly and Curtis Turner would rent a hotel room and party all night and drink until daylight. Then they'd both go out and drive a 500-mile race. But Lorenzen would be out in the parking lot with the headlights of his rental car on so he could work on his race car to get it ready for the race the next day.

I only remember having one run-in with Lorenzen during his career. It was a little more physical than I had counted on.

I was in the pits at Daytona in 1962. The drivers would shut their engines off just before they came into the pits so they could get plug checks, just like they do today.

The cars would come down pit road and you wouldn't hear them coming at all. They were silent but still going rather fast. That was the first thing I learned at a race track: Never turn your back on the race cars and always make sure you know where they are.

I started across the opening, and I looked and there wasn't anything coming. I got about halfway across and someone yelled to me and I turned around to see who it was, and the next thing I knew I was flying through the air.

Fred had been doing a plug check and had his engine off. He whipped through that opening and didn't see me, and he was suddenly right there. He ran into my behind and just brushed me, really.

It threw me about five or six feet, and I dropped my tape recorder and busted it all to pieces. I skinned my hands and knees but I was really OK. I jumped up and brushed myself off like I was cool and it was no big deal. People came rushing up and asked me if I was hurt, but I said I was OK.

A few minutes later, Fred came back out to where I was standing. He said, "Who did I run into out here a few minutes ago?'

Someone said, "You hit this boy right here." He looked at me and he said, "Are you OK?"

I said, "Yeah, I guess."

"Well, you ought to watch where the hell you're going!"

And he turned around and walked off.

And he was right. I should have,

21

DAVID THE BROADCASTER

Some of the very best broadcasters in the business are those who have actually turned speeds exceeding 200 miles per hour as well as engaged in some rather fierce fender-to-fender battles that often leave quite a bit of sheet metal damage. They understand what a driver feels, what a car is doing, why particular moves either work or fail on the race track. They bring a great deal of information to the fans that may otherwise be overlooked or misdiagnosed.

I thought that David Pearson would be perfect for the job.

It took some persuasion, but I finally got David to agree to do a television broadcast back in the early 1990s. He had already retired from driving, and as I tried to explain to him, I thought he had the potential of becoming a rather interesting person in the booth because he had so much experience. David certainly didn't disappoint me.

I think David could have been a great broadcaster but he just never had a burning desire to do it after he retired in 1989. Some of the folks at ESPN came to me and asked me why I thought he kept turning them down. Knowing David like I do, I said David just wasn't interested in doing that. Doing television just wasn't his thing. He had no desire to be in front of a camera, even when he was racing.

Buddy Baker came to me one time right after he started doing some television stuff with them and asked, "Can you get David to come up to Rockingham this weekend and at least sit in the booth with us? They'll pay him some pretty good money, so see if he likes the idea." I told Buddy I would.

I called him and told him about the offer. He said there was no way he was going to do that. I told him to come up and try it, and he might like it. So finally he agreed to do it.

The day came, and David went into the booth with them. We had a television monitor in our radio booth, and I was watching him, and he was doing a pretty good job. I turned the sound up in our booth during our commercial breaks, and he was bringing out some good points.

Somewhere in the telecast, Baker said, "David, you had great success with the Wood Brothers over the years. How many races did you and the Wood Brothers win here at Rockingham?" David said, "Buddy, to be honest with you, I don't remember." Baker said, "Pearson, there ain't a race driver on earth that doesn't know every race he's ever won. I can tell you every race I've ever won." David looked at him and said, "Well, Buddy, if I hadn't won any more than you did, I could, too!"

Baker went into total shock right there on camera.

22

PROBLEM NOTED

I n the days before NASCAR racing became a nationally recognized sport, relationships between driver and crew were much more laid back than today. A complete pit crew in the 1960s and '70s might have only consisted of six people or eight people, unlike the 70 or 80 or more found on today's top tcams.

Practice sessions in NASCAR in the early 1970s were much less structured than they are today, often to the point where the entire crew might not even stay around while the driver was on the track.

Sometimes the crew would leave the race track before the practice sessions were over, aside from maybe one crew member left to button down the car. If they did, the driver would sometimes leave a note on the dashboard or in the seat regarding what he wanted fixed the next morning before he got back to the track for the next practice. Some of the things left on those notes were pretty funny.

I remember some incidences that happened with Bud Moore's team when Bobby Isaac and Bobby Allison drove for him. The crew came in one morning and there was a note on the seat. The note read, "Something loose under the hood." The crew would put notes back in the seat for the driver when he got in the car. Someone on the crew would write, "Something under the hood tightened." There would be another note another day from the driver that read, "Right rear tire almost worn out." The crew would leave one that said, "Checked the right rear. Almost replaced it."

There was a note left once dealing with the two-way radio. The note from the driver read, "Static is unbelievably loud in the headset." The note from the crew the next morning read, "Fixed the headset. The noise is now believable."

We simply don't have nearly as much fun in the sport these days as we used to.

23

OH HENRY

There are many personalities among crew members in NASCAR Nextel Cup racing. Some are quiet and calculating, only thinking of the race car and the job at hand. Others see the sport as their own personal playground, and they, too, can be quite serious when a win is on the line. But before that respective checkered flag falls, there's plenty of mischief that goes on around the race track. Many times, the friendly gouging is applied to those who least suspect it.

One of those fun-loving individuals is Henry Benfield, a longtime crewman for various teams owners including Junior Johnson, Rick Hendrick, and Larry McClure and Morgan-McClure Racing, to name a few.

There are probably a thousand stories involving Henry, and I would guess maybe 950 of them are unprintable. Henry's smile doesn't always say, "Have a good day." There's a good bet he may be up to something. Henry worked a lot of years for Junior Johnson and his drivers, such as Cale Yarborough, Darrell Waltrip, Neil Bonnett, and Terry Labonte.

Henry was and still is one of the sport's true characters, and I have to say my first encounter with Henry was not good. Henry was working for Junior way back when, as they say, and he called me up on the team transporter one afternoon. Ole' Henry had a big platter of chocolate chip cookies made. I'm a nut for chocolate chip cookies anyway, and I said, "Hey Henry, do you care if I have a couple of your cookies?" Henry stuttered when he got excited and said, "No-no t-t-t-take all the cookies you want. Those th-th-th-things are good." What I didn't know, but other people did, was that Henry was a heck of a cook. Problem was he baked those cookies with a pretty good dose of Ex-Lax. I ate about four or five of them, and you can imagine what happened over the next few hours.

He had them on the truck until everybody found out what he was doing. I saw Henry a couple of races later, and he said, "Hey Barney, c-c-c-come here. I've got s-s-some more cookies!" I said, "Man, I don't want any more of your cookies." He said, "Them cookies are for people on th-th-th-the run. Get you a handful of them!" I said, "No way, Henry! No way!"

I learned over the years that if Henry offered me anything on Junior's truck, forget it! There was a trick or prank attached to it.

There was also a time when one of the Miss Winston ladies was brand new to the sport and went on the truck to meet everyone. T. Wayne Robertson and Ralph Seagraves, who were both executives with NASCAR's first series sponsor, R.J. Reynolds Tobacco Co. T. Wayne and Ralph were taking her around the garage introducing her to everyone. This young lady asked for a couple of cookies, but before T. Wayne and Ralph could stop her or say anything, she had gobbled down a couple of them. So they just looked at each other and let her keep on going. Well, needless to say, no one saw her for the next three or four days.

Henry was so bad about doctoring a variety of things that he got the nickname, "Dr. Benfield."

If a guard at a gate gave Henry a hard time about credentials or whatever and was particularly obnoxious to him, Henry would go back and apologize to him and say, "You know, I-I-I'm sorry a-a-a-about that run-in we had. I-I-I'm going to bring you some good cold lemonade since it's so h-h-h hot out here." The guard would forgive him and would anticipate that cold lemonade coming his way later in the day. Naturally, Henry couldn't resist doing his best work and would put Croatian oil in it, which is something worse than castor oil. Lord knows what else he would put in it, and pretty soon there'd be a guard change on that gate, and you wouldn't ever see the guy again. He'd drink a couple of tall glasses of the stuff and you wouldn't see him for the rest of the weekend.

I remember another trick Henry would often play that would usually turn men into mice and caused more than one person to think they were going to have a heart attack.

Henry was notorious for carrying a rubber snake in a box. It was black and big and pretty scary looking the first time you peeked through the flaps to get a glimpse of what was in there. Henry would look around for anybody who was afraid of snakes. That meant a driver, crew member, NASCAR official, whomever.

It seemed like the characters who were most susceptible to being terrified of anything that resembled a snake were working for Bud Moore, a longtime team owner in NASCAR in the early 1960s through a good part of the 1990s.

There were two crewmen Henry would get the best of. One was Harold Stott, and in recent years, a boy named Phil Thomas. Harold was terrified of snakes. You could throw a shoe string and he would crawl over 40 people to get out of the truck.

When we first started going to Sears Point, California, in the early 1990s, Henry was staying at the same hotel where Harold was staying. Henry went into the hotel early one afternoon and told the desk clerk he had a package for a guest named Harold Stott. He told the desk clerk he was supposed to find Harold at the track but couldn't find him. Henry said, "I've got to get ready to go out to dinner, so can I just leave the box in his room? You let me have the key, and I'll just put it on the bed so he'll see it." So, after some heavy persuasion, the clerk finally gave him the key.

Henry went in the room and hid, and Harold came in not too long after that from a long day at the track. Henry waited until he got in the shower and once he heard the water running and was sure he was in there, Henry pulled the shower curtain back, put the rubber snake around his neck and said, "Here, Harold, hold this!"

Harold saw that snake and tore the shower curtain down, went out the door, ran into the hall and halfway down to the front desk just as naked as the day he was born before he ever realized what was going on. The hotel clerk was going to call the sheriff because they couldn't figure out why Harold was running around in his birthday suit.

Had it been me, I believe I would have shot Ole' Henry. I don't know for sure, but it wouldn't surprise me if Henry's been shot at least a half-dozen times for all the pranks he's pulled over the years.

24

THE PEA PICKER

Aside from snakes and spiked cookies, Henry Benfield was also pretty big into the CB radio craze of the 1970s. Benfield worked as a transporter driver in the '70s and '80s and was just as unpredictable on the roads as he was around the garage area.

Henry was just as crazy away from the race track as he was around it, often ignoring the speed limit signs altogether. But he wasn't the only one doing that. With a busy race schedule that criss-crossed the country, transporter drivers often would, as they say, "Put the pedal to the metal."

Henry once told me a story concerning one of his many trips across the country.

Back when CB radios were the hot item in the 1970s, there were all kinds of CB stories floating around. The transporter drivers still use CB radios even today, and they help them get around and stay in touch with each other if someone has some type of mechanical breakdown.

The transporter drivers usually run together pretty often en route to the race tracks. They run that way partly because they have someone to talk to, and also to never be alone on the highway.

The transporter drivers would often run six and eight trucks in a pack. There would always be a point guy out in front who would say it's clear, it's this, it's that, or whatever.

They were going to Ontario, California, one time for a race at the Ontario Motor Speedway, a track that's no longer there. It was a long trip from North Carolina where most of the teams are based, and it took days to get there. Of course, everyone had what they call a CB handle, a name they used from radio to radio. The handle that Henry chose was "Pea Picker."

Henry was barreling down through Arizona, leading this convoy of race trucks. Henry got on the microphone and said, "Breaker 1-9. This is 'ole Pea Picker. Come on up, boys, it's real clear and you can see for 10 miles. There ain't nothing out here but the stars and the moon. It's clean and green. Just run what you want to run."

So Henry was barreling on down the road and he dove under an overpass and all of a sudden a voice came over the CB radio. The voice asked, "Hey, Pea Picker, do you copy?" Henry said, "10-4, good buddy. Wh-Wh-Wh-Who am I talking to?"

The voice said, "Hey, good buddy. This is Arizona state trooper Roy Johnson. I've got you at about 90 miles per hour in a 55 zone. Why don't you just pull off down here at the foot of the hill. And I'd like to invite all of your friends running whatever they want to run to come down here and join you."

Then Trooper Johnson added one more thought. He said, "Oh, and Pea Picker, I just want you to know your peas have just been picked!"

25

EARL COMES OFF HIS HINGES

Each time NASCAR travels to a particular part of the country, hotel rates seem to have a way of rising dramatically. Some hotel operators realize everyone needs a place to stay when NASCAR drivers, teams, and fans are in town, and they are unfortunately often at their mercy.

I remember one incident where one well-respected person in the sport had finally had enough and wasn't going to take it anymore.

We were in Riverside, California, in the mid-1970s and had only been going out there for a couple of years. Riverside International Raceway was a road course that is no longer on the NASCAR schedule. As a matter of fact, the track isn't even there any longer. Someone bought the land it was sitting on and turned the area into a huge housing development.

When we were there for races, we all stayed at the Holiday Inn in Riverside, and a lot of times back then, drivers, teams, and the media would stay in the same hotel together. Drivers didn't have the nice million-dollar motor coaches that they pack in the infield now.

On this particular weekend in January, we had been there a few days, and the Sunday morning of the race, all of the race people went down to the front desk to check out. All week long, there had been this big sign out front on the marquee advertising that the rooms were $49 a night. When we turned in our keys, everyone checking out was being told that the rooms had been jacked up to $100 a night. A lot of people were raising the devil about it, but the manager refused to change it.

I was standing there at the front desk, along with several other media members and a driver or two, when a gentleman by the name of Earl Parker walked up. Earl worked with Champion Spark Plugs for years as their track representative, and if you had any type of plug-related engine problem, he was the man to talk to. When Earl got word of the rate increase, he hit the ceiling.

Earl said, "Forget it! I'm not going to pay it. The sign says $49 a night, and I'm paying $49." The person behind the desk said, "Well, we'll just call the sheriff, and you won't be able to get your luggage out of the room until you pay it." Earl said, "Well, we'll see about that!" He turned and marched to the elevator, pushed the button and went back to his room.

Earl was one of our good friends, and we picked on him all the time. We had a lot of fun with Earl, like the time we told him the higher the number on his golf balls, the farther they would go down the fairway. We let him dig all the high-numbered balls out of his bag before Pearson and I finally told him it wasn't true. So when this situation at the hotel developed, we were laughing our butts off. We were sitting there on the lobby sofa watching everything unfold. David elbowed me and said, "We know Earl, so let's see what happens here."

Earl stepped out of the elevator carrying his hotel room door. On that door was a little placard underneath a piece of plexiglass, and on that card were the posted nightly rates. At that time, you couldn't charge any more than what was posted on the door, according to California law.

Earl went to the desk and had the door in his hands, and the desk clerk was going berserk. The desk clerk said, "What are you doing with our door?"

Earl said, "I want to show you something."

The desk clerk said, "That's it! I'm calling the sheriff! You're destroying our room!" Earl said, "You go ahead and call the sheriff, because he needs to see this, too!" Earl welcomed the idea because he knew he was right. He asked, "What does that say right there on that placard?" The desk clerk said, "It says $49 dollars a night." Earl said, "Go ahead and call the sheriff. Then you can tell him you're robbing everybody who is staying here."

Then Earl took the door, went back up to the room, put the door back on its hinges and came back down. Earl Parker paid $49 a night for the room, and so did everybody else who stayed there that weekend. He was the one who scored racing's victory that day!

26

TOUGH OL' CALE

When Cale Yarborough entered the world of NASCAR in 1958, the first impression he gave to all in the garage area was his absolute need to succeed as a driver and a champion.

Some of the stories that surround Cale Yarborough's life and career are nothing short of amazing. Cale is from Timmonsville, South Carolina, a small town just down the way from Darlington. He has been struck by lightning, came close to drowning in a pond while wrestling an alligator, wrestled bears, crash landed an airplane and has been bitten by a rattlesnake. And as the story goes, the rattlesnake died.

And, oh yeah, he raced stock cars at 210 miles per hour. On the race track, Cale proved his toughness after flipping cars at both Daytona and Darlington and lived to tell about it. Ironically, his best success came on those tracks. He won four Daytona 500s and five Southern 500s at Darlington.

Cale Yarborough, driver of the Junior Johnson-owned Chevrolets, addresses the fans after accepting the trophy for one of his many wins at Bristol, Tennessee in the mid-1970s. Hall presented many trophies to the South Carolina native.
Photo by Randy Powell

He won 83 races over 30 years, and in 1976, '77 and '78, he was crowned NASCAR Winston Cup champion and is still the only man to ever win three consecutive titles.

His career began in 1958 when he crawled under a fence at Darlington to get in the garage area to slide undetected behind the wheel of a friend's race car. That is, until Norris Friel, NASCAR's technical director, discovered he was too young to drive and was without a NASCAR license. Friel proceeded to throw him out three or four times. I think Friel had the sheriff eventually escort him off the premises.

Yarborough retired from driving in 1988 and turned his attention to team ownership for the next decade or so. Unfortunately, he didn't enjoy the same success as an owner that he had as a driver.

I've personally known Cale since the early 1960s and watched him emerge into one of NASCAR's great legends. Cale was a tough little race car driver. There was no other way to describe him. In his own mind, he felt like he could beat anybody coming or going. In the early days, that included great drivers like Jack Smith, Fireball Roberts, Joe Weatherly, or anybody who had raced at Darlington Raceway or anywhere else for that matter. He felt like that when he was 15 years old. He told me once how he just knew he could drive a race car as well as anyone. And he did.

I've had a very good relationship with Cale over the years because he was Junior Johnson's driver for a lot of those years, and I'm still close with Junior. I've never met anyone who was as determined to win races or finish in the top five as Cale was.

There were two reasons for that. One, Cale liked the dollar bill and still does, as we all do, I guess. Aside from that, whether they would have paid him or not, he would have been one of those guys like the late Dale Earnhardt. He would have driven a race car if he had to pay money to race.

The thing about Cale was that he probably knew less about a race car than two-thirds of the guys who ever sat down in one. That didn't make any difference. If the car was loose, pushing or whatever, he would tell the crew that. He would say, "That thing won't turn" or "The rear end feels like it's going to spin out," or "The rear wheels are spinning and not gripping in the turns." And he'd walk off. He wouldn't tell them to put a certain spring in it or shorten the sway bar. He'd just walk away. Sometimes they'd fix it, and other times they'd have no clue what to do to it and they didn't do anything. But they'd tell him what they tried. Junior Johnson can confirm that and so would a dozen other drivers.

If the car wasn't right or was a 15th-place car, he could win with it or finish in the top five. That's how hard he would drive it.

When I was broadcasting from the turns, I would see him come by me, and he would look like a gorilla trying to twist the steering wheel off that thing to keep it between the walls. I've seen that man get out of a car with blisters all over his hands. Sometimes they would break and there would be blood running from both hands. He'd still take that car and win a race with it.

I remember once one of his crew guys told me they were having trouble with a buzz in the two-way radio. For a while there, it kept happening every week. They worked on it and worked on it and finally figured out what it was. Cale didn't know it, but his hand was keying the mike on the steering wheel tightly, and the buzz they were hearing was Cale grunting as he was trying to hang on to the race car in the turns. And the cars back in the '70s were big and bulky and didn't have power steering like they have today. These drivers today couldn't drive the cars that Cale and Bobby Allison and Buddy Baker and Pearson and even Junior drove before them. They honest to goodness couldn't. The forearms on some of those guys were huge from hanging on to the race cars week in and week out.

I've had some television broadcast guys come along and ask me how to get Cale to talk. I would tell them to make him mad, and you'll get an answer.

You could ask Cale reasonable questions, and he would only say, "Yes" or "No" or "Yeah boy, that's right." Cale just wouldn't open up and talk with you. I think it was just a lack of self-confidence in the early days.

Back in the '60s and '70s, there weren't too many guys who liked to get in front of a camera or in front of a group of people to speak at all. If you listen to some of the interviews I have from back then, they're pretty rough.

I remember the day Cale drove a Banjo Matthews-owned Ford out of Darlington Raceway on Labor Day in 1965. I found myself a little closer to the action than I normally liked.

I was there that day in Darlington when he sailed out of the race track. I wasn't on the air that day, but I was in that old open-air press box they used to have there. The only thing protecting the media was some old chicken wire stretched over the front of it. If Cale had been about 30 more feet to the right, he would have taken out the whole press box. I was there to see the race, and I did some interviews for my sports show on WIFM radio there in Elkin.

When I saw him climbing back up the bank and crossing the wall to get back into the race track, the race was still going on but under caution. I didn't realize it was him. We all jumped up and went around the corner so we could see how bad his car was. There were dozens of people around the car wanting to know if he was hurt. We all sat back down, and the next thing I knew, there was Cale. He was standing there at the old guard rail and when he got a break in the traffic, he went on across and went back to the garage. I remember he was combing his hair the whole time as he was making his way back.

When Cale got back down to the pits, he found Banjo. Before Banjo could ask him what happened, Cale said, "Banjo, I think I bent your car."

27

A RIP-ROARING GOOD TIME

n earlier days of NASCAR racing, track schedules seemed to go on forever. At one point in NASCAR history, qualifying for the Labor Day Southern 500 event could take as many as two weeks to complete. The idea was that more time spent on the track meant more opportunities for coverage in local newspapers. It was great coverage leading up to the 500-mile race on Labor Day.

With all of that down time, a lot of us were forced to make the best of the situation. I enjoyed using the public address microphone to my advantage.

I had a good friend named Dick Beaty. I thought the world of Dick. He was once a driver in NASCAR in the early 1950s and then went on to become a NASCAR official for many, many years. He became what was then known as the NASCAR Winston Cup Director and held that job for many years. Unfortunately, he passed away several years ago, and I really miss him.

I was always making announcements on the public address system. I did P.A. work at almost every track we went to in the days leading up to race day. I was always announcing that Dick should go to the back gate to see someone who was there to meet him. A lot of those times nobody was there, but he was never sure, so he'd have to go and check anyway. Sometimes I would say stuff like, "Dick Beaty. Report to the back gate. Your dentist is here to deliver your teeth!" It was a good way to relieve the boredom between practice and qualifying.

Well, there was one time I guess it all caught up with me. We were at Martinsville Speedway for a race, and I needed to get outside the track down in turn one to go back to where our broadcast booth was. Beaty was getting ready to turn the cars loose in practice. Back then, there wasn't a tunnel that ran under turn four as there is now. Up until two or three years ago, you had to wait until the track was clear to get in or out of the race track. So you had to always remember everything you needed for the race, or you weren't going to get it. The only way they would throw a caution was to allow an ambulance out of the track in the event of an emergency with a driver or a fan. It was something that happened on rare occasions. It had to be something really important to throw a caution flag, especially during a race.

So on this particular day, they had already closed the crossover gate and I couldn't get out. Beaty was standing there on pit road. I went to him and told him how badly I needed to get out. He said, "I'll tell you what I'll do. I'll hold the cars for just a minute and you run down to turn one, and that gate is opened down there. You can go through that gate and go right on up to the tower." So I went flying down pit road toward turn one. I had a tape recorder in one hand and a notebook in the other. I got over there, and believe it or not, the gate was locked.

And wouldn't you know it, about the time I got across the track, Beaty turned the cars loose. There were 30 or 40 race cars out there running, and I was standing there between the fence and the race track. I knew I needed to get out of there, but I didn't know how I was going to do it because I was trapped. I don't know to this day if Beaty tricked me or if the gate was locked by accident, but you could say he got me back.

I thought, "What the heck, I'll just climb over the fence." So I climbed up the fence and there were two strands of barbwire on top of it. I finally got up there and I got one leg over one side and I had one leg over the other, and I caught the rear of my pants on the fence. And the worst part was I couldn't get loose and I couldn't go either way. Being a practice session, there were probably two or three thousand people in the grandstands.

Beaty was up in the tower and he saw me down there struggling to move. So he picked up the microphone to the P.A. and in his high voice said, "Ladies and gentlemen, I would like to introduce Barney Hall, the track announcer. That's him hung on the fence down there in turn one!" They all stood up and gave me a big round of applause. I was so embarrassed, I just didn't know what to do. I just gave my pants a big tug and ripped the whole rear end of my britches out. I walked on up through the stands and waved and everybody was laughing. I'm telling you, it was a hell of a day!

28

MY FRIEND MARTY

O ne of my good friends was the late Marty Robbins, an award-winning country music singer who also possessed a great deal of talent behind the controls of a race car. While others raced for a living, Robbins did so as a hobby of sorts, enjoying every minute spent in any garage area. While other entertainers toured the world for relaxation, Robbins found relaxation around his race cars, occasionally qualifying for races at superspeedways like Daytona and Talladega.

Marty began driving race cars on a local level around his Nashville, Tennessee home in the early 1960s and would follow NASCAR events by newspaper and radio for the next decade. By the mid-1970s, he began hanging around the garage area and finally got the bug to run a few NASCAR Winston Cup events. Marty bought Dodges from Cotton Owens and Bobby Allison when he got the urge to race in NASCAR events. All told, Robbins drove in 14 events from 1975 until 1982, collecting $20,105 in winnings.

Often Robbins could be found in restaurants around the tracks, giving impromptu free concerts for fans who were in town for races. Little time would pass before the entire place would be rocking. Marty would purposely seek out restaurants, such as pizza joints or even some of the finer establishments that had pianos on the premises. When the clock would finally work its way toward closing time, Robbins would usually offer to buy the piano, move it to the parking lot, and keep on playing. On a few occasions, when the manager would tell him it was closing time, he offered to buy the restaurant just so he could keep the music flowing.

There were many gold records hanging on his walls during his illustrious entertainment career. He brought a great deal of joy to an adoring public, both through music and racing.

By the late 1970s, heart problems curtailed his trips to the race tracks. Marty died in 1982 of a massive heart attack.

Marty was a great country music singer with a beautiful voice, but he could have been just as good as a comedian. It's hard to believe we lost Marty over 20 years ago. I remember how sad everyone in the sport was when the news of his passing spread through the garage area. He was very well liked among his competitors as well as among the media and the fans.

He was close friends with Hoss Ellington, a longtime team owner in NASCAR who had several prominent drivers in his cars, including Cale Yarborough and Donnie Allison. Marty and Hoss would often trade jokes and try to "one up" each other. We were in Talladega one summer and Hoss was talking about how dry it had been. Hoss said, "It's so dry up where I live, I've got fish six weeks old that don't even know how to swim." Marty would say, "That ain't nothing. In Nashville, it's so dry we're catching catfish and they have ticks on 'em." They were always trying to outdo each other.

Marty began coming around when we started going to the old Nashville race track when they held NASCAR Grand National events there. Before he started racing, he would run some celebrity races and some short track races around Nashville, and he really liked driving. Deep down, Marty wanted to be a race car driver maybe more so than a singer. That was a true passion with him. He was a heck of a lot better race car driver than people gave him credit for.

Cotton Owens, a longtime team owner in the sport, built him some good race cars, and a lot of times he would qualify in the top 10 or 15 and could race there, but he knew he couldn't do it for 500 miles. But it just tickled him to death to get out there and run the first 200 miles, make pit stops, and the whole nine yards. But if guys were really serious about maybe winning or they were in the points battle and they were running close to him, he also knew he needed to get out of the way and let them go.

Another one of Marty's good friends was Joe Frasson, a driver who fielded his own Dodges for many years. Marty and Joe used to bet each other on who would qualify better. This went back and forth for several races. Finally, to get Joe's goat, Marty had Cotton build him a big motor for the car that he was going to run at Talladega. Cotton asked him what he was going to do if he got caught. Marty said, "I'll pay the fine. It'll be worth every penny just to see the look on Joe's face." Marty knew Joe wasn't a very good loser.

So on qualifying day Marty went out and laid down a really fast lap, and Joe was stunned. It didn't take long for NASCAR to put two and two together and realize something was up. But for just a few minutes, Marty had him. As expected, NASCAR fined him for the big motor. Marty laughed the whole time he was paying it.

He was like that. If he wanted to win a bet or wanted to do something outrageous like drive race cars, he would find a way to get it done. He was a lot of fun to hang out with.

29

THE BOASTFUL DARRELL WALTRIP

When Darrell Waltrip came into NASCAR Winston Cup racing in 1975, he did so with the mentality that he could outrun and outdrive anyone on the race track. He sang hard and loud that he was going to be the next superstar on the circuit and that everyone else needed to move over and make room.

Darrell simply came to NASCAR racing like a hurricane out of control. Few people were impressed with his boastful comments, especially established drivers like Cale Yarborough, David Pearson, Richard Petty, Bobby Allison, and Buddy Baker, those who were winning virtually all the races at the time.

When Waltrip addressed the media, they were just as shocked as the drivers at the comments the Owensboro, Kentucky native was making. I remember raising more than one eyebrow over some of the predictions Waltrip made.

When his career came to a conclusion at the end of the 2000 NASCAR season, Waltrip had emerged as one of the sport's all-time biggest stars with three NASCAR championships and 84 career victories. Further, he went on to become one of the most respected individuals in the garage area. He took his vast knowledge of stock car racing to the airwaves, enjoying a stellar television broadcasting career.

Darrell was outspoken from day one. My first memory of Darrell was during a golf tournament at Darlington in 1974 or '75. Quite a few of the media people were playing in that tournament back in those days. He was talking to everybody about 90 miles per hour and serving notice that he could beat the best. Needless to say, that just set everybody on fire.

The weird thing was within a span of a year, when he got a decent ride, he backed up what he said. And that made everybody madder than they already were.

I compare Darrell Waltrip to maybe a Tim Richmond when he showed up in 1982 as the new kid on the block. He had a good bit of success, and the oldtimers resented it real quick. They hated to hear him talk because he could go out and back it up.

Some of the most thrilling moments I've ever had in racing— broadcasting or watching—were with Darrell Waltrip at Talladega. I remember one time not many years ago when he was kind of bad-mouthing the young guys, saying they were driving reckless and crazy and how they weren't using their heads. I can remember back in the late 1970s and early 1980s when he had a good race car when he drove for Junior Johnson. Some other teams talked about him making some crazy moves. He made them work, and he won races by doing it.

I also remember one time in 1983 at Talladega when Waltrip was having a difficult afternoon. He had been battling for the championship, but on this particular day his car simply wouldn't get up to speed.

I was doing a piece with Junior for the radio. At that time of the season, Darrell had been running pretty hot and was going for his third consecutive title. They had won maybe six out of the last 10 races, but when they got to Talladega, they were running very badly.

I was interviewing Junior in the media center and other reporters were around. We were talking about how bad the car was and what was going on that they weren't running any better. The car stayed out there, but they were two or three laps down.

I asked Junior if there was something wrong with the car or with Darrell. Junior said, "Constipation." That threw me for a flip. I thought, "What in the devil is he doing? Is he pulling my leg or what?" I had to have some kind of comeback, so all I could say was, "What do you mean constipation?" Junior said, "Well, it has to be either the car or the driver, because neither one of them passed a thing all day long." I just about fell out of my chair laughing, but Junior was good about that. You never knew what you were going to get with him.

30

GOING TO THE BOOTH

Joe Moore, the entire MRN broadcast crew, and I have comprised "the voice of NASCAR" over the past decade. We are a close group with a huge amount of respect for one another.

But becoming "the voice of NASCAR" in the booth wasn't something I was looking forward to in the beginning.

I was scared to death the first time I did the booth. I begged Jim Foster (then the head of MRN) not to put me in the booth. I told him in no uncertain terms that I didn't want to be in the booth.

But to be quite frank with you, the only reason I'm in the booth today is because Foster told me I would work the booth or I wouldn't work. I thought to myself that I didn't want to get out of racing, so I had to give in. I didn't have a choice.

I went in the booth and everyone tried to help me. I had five people writing notes to me because Foster said he would put several people in there to slip me notes. They were slipping notes under my nose right and left. Finally I said, "Tell them not to hand me anything. Let me look out the window and try this on my own." That's the way I work today. If you can't look out that window and relay what's going on, you've got a problem.

One thing that stands out in my mind almost my first race in the booth was than a little extra unexpected excitement. So many people today remember the 1979 Daytona 500 more for the postrace fight between Cale Yarborough, Bobby Allison, and Donnie Allison than they do the race. It happened at the end of the race after Cale and Donnie crashed while going for the win.

There have been plenty of fights around race tracks over the years, especially on the short tracks. But what made this fight so memorable was that it was the first race CBS Sports had broadcast and it was national flag-to-flag coverage. It was just so unexpected and a highlight to a wild race that ultimately featured Richard Petty winning his sixth of seven Daytona 500s.

Part of the story was that Petty had just had major stomach surgery a week before the race and had ignored his doctor's advice not to drive.

I don't think anyone had ever seen a fight like that after such a high-exposure race. A lot of folks weren't even aware it was going on until it was over at the bottom of turn three. Once the word spread around the race track, that was all everybody was talking about. I don't think anyone at that point cared who won the race. They were all talking about the fight over in turn three. From my vantage point there in the booth, I really couldn't see what was going on. I did see the cars slide to the bottom of the track. CBS had a television monitor and I looked over and could see people grabbing and pushing one another. Our turn guy was calling in that there was a fight at the apron of the race track. But he didn't say who it was for a minute, so it took a while to soak in what was really going on.

What started the whole deal was that Cale and Donnie had gotten into each other pretty heavily coming down the backstretch on the last lap.

That put both of them in the wall with a lot of damage to their cars and they couldn't make it back. Donnie and Cale were discussing the situation and Bobby stopped over there to offer Donnie a ride back to

Just prior to going on the air at Martinsville (Virginia) Speedway, Hall is captured for the camera along with MRN executive producer John McMullen (standing) and fellow booth announcer Mike Joy in 1984. *Motorsports Images & Archives. Used with permission.*

the garage. They way Bobby tells it, Cale popped him in the face with his helmet and Bobby wasn't going to stand for that.

In the end, fines were passed out and eventually everything was settled. Even though that was nearly 30 years ago, it's still a sore subject for the three of them to talk about.

A lot of people thought the fight was going to give NASCAR a black eye, so to speak, but I think it actually helped to launch NASCAR into prime time. That's what the race fans and most everyone around the country talked about for the next two weeks. It was widely viewed because there was a heavy snowstorm that blanketed the entire east coast that weekend and people found themselves trapped in front of their televisions.

Working the booth is quite different from working a turn or pit road. Being in the booth means having to work all facets of the race and not just one portion of it when called upon.

When you're in the turn you can kind of watch the race like a fan would and do a good job broadcasting the action. You can't do that in the booth, because it's work. I do enjoy the booth, especially when it's raining and cold. But some of the best fun I've ever had was while I was working the turns.

In the garage you can formulate a story and have time to develop it. But in any other area you have to say something. Even if you make it up, you have to say something. You can't just stand there, waiting for something to happen. Some of our best announcers started in the turns and in the pits, and I did the turns for a long time.

While there have been a few shocking moments on the track, I've also been surprised a few times in the booth itself.

We have a panel underneath the counter in the broadcast booth. If your volume goes up or down you have a little switch under there so you can adjust the volume in your earpiece. That's a standard thing that's has been part of the broadcast for a while. We were at one of the race tracks and they had just rewired the booth. We had just come on the air, and the volume was breaking up a little bit. I reached under the counter for that switch to turn it down, and there was an electric wire that wasn't attached to anything but it did have power to it. I was talking on the air and reaching for this volume control and instead touched the wire and probably got 110 volts shot up my rear end. I won't tell you what I said out loud, but it did go out on the air. That was a shock in more ways than one.

When I'm in the booth, I really get into watching the races, especially when the action is exciting. There have been times when I've wanted to just watch the race instead of having to broadcast it.

There have been plenty of times when I've stood up for the finishes and even do so now. There were a lot of years when I would want to turn around to whoever was in the booth with me and say, "You do the next three laps. I want to watch this."

31

IRONHEAD DALE EARNHARDT

There's no question seven-time NASCAR champion Dale Earnhardt was one of the most respected drivers in all of the sport's history. Much of that respect obviously came from his phenomenal talent on the race track, often mixed with a rough driving style that prompted some drivers to crash just trying to get out of his way. Bobby Allison takes credit for dubbing him "Ironhead" in the late 1980s for routinely bumping and pushing his way to victory.

An equal portion of the respect he received was because he came from humble beginnings, made his lifelong dream a reality, and became one of the very best drivers to ever turn the wheel of a stock car.

Behind his "man in black" persona and "Intimidator" label was a common man who could relate to the real trials of life. He had lived in house trailers without heat and kitchens with no food. In the early days, he had to win on the short tracks because the money he borrowed from the bank on Friday had to be paid back on Monday. There was no finishing second. He would lose the race car and everything else he owned that he put up for collateral if he lost. He would lose everything, even though he hardly had anything to lose.

When Earnhardt came to NASCAR for a few races in 1975, he possessed so much talent that it needed to be harnessed and polished and channeled in a positive direction. And when it came to social skills, he was greatly lacking there as well. Dale was a country boy who had not experienced a great deal of exposure outside of Cabarrus County.

In 1979, Earnhardt joined California businessman Rod Osterland full time with his new team and won his first NASCAR Winston Cup race at Bristol Motor Speedway in August of that year. He collected enough rookie points to win Rookie of the Year by season's end.

The next season, he won again at Atlanta, Bristol, and Charlotte and was crowned NASCAR Winston Cup champion. He didn't feel he was secure as a fixture in the sport. That didn't come until several years later when with championship No. 2 in 1986 and No. 3 in 1987 he felt he had a place in NASCAR Winston Cup racing as long as he wanted it.

Team owners Richard Childress, J.D. Stacy, and Bud Moore called on Earnhardt for his driving services before he and Childress reunited a second time in 1984. They produced four more championships between 1990 and 1994, and Earnhardt had seven, just like Richard. All told, Earnhardt also collected 76 career victories. But despite all of his success, he never lost sight of where he came from. Earnhardt never forgot those who helped him along the way.

Dale started off with nothing when he raced short tracks and in his first year or two in NASCAR Winston Cup competition. No matter how much money he made, I don't think it ever changed him. Yes, he lost some money in the early 1980s when he first started winning big money. There were a few investments that he made that didn't really pan out, but once he gained some knowledge about how to invest, he was a smart businessman.

I think Dale did finally realize what type of power he had in the sport. He never used his power to hurt anyone, but he did realize how that power could help the entire sport. There were times when he would go to NASCAR about a certain rule they were thinking about implementing and tell them how he felt it might hurt the sport. He was about the only one who could go up in the NASCAR truck and do that. He had an incredible gift for seeing the big picture. And the majority of the time, he was right. NASCAR would listen to him.

I enjoyed a close friendship with Dale, often spending time with him when we were away from the track. We enjoyed each other's company, especially since he could be himself around me, and he would often come to my house there in the mountains around Elkin to simply escape from the pressures of racing.

Like so many other drivers, Dale and I became friends through radio interviews he sat down for around the race track.

I started traveling with Dale when he first came into the sport in 1978 when he started running a few more NASCAR Winston Cup races. I was always proud of the fact I had taken him under my wing since I had been around the business a long time and he had a lot of confidence in me. He would ask me questions about what to do and what not to do, and what to say and what not to say. The man had a ton of personalities. Some were good and some were bad. Some were indifferent. But above all, he had a heart of gold.

Dale came to Elkin fairly regularly around 1981 and '82, and I was piddling in older model Ford Mustangs back then. He would come up and help me work on my old cars. And sometimes he would come up and get beans and other vegetables out of my garden. Even though he was already a champion by then, he'd put on his old jeans and T-shirts and fill five-gallon buckets with beans just like anybody else. He was just a normal guy who never forgot his roots.

When I needed some help with my house, I asked Dale to help me find the one item that would give it that cozy home feel. When I built my house, I was looking for some old brick, and I asked him one day if he knew where I could find some. He said, "Yeah, we've leased a place in South Carolina from a pulp wood company, and that's where we hunt deer. There are a lot of old places that have dilapidated chimneys that are falling in. If you want to follow me down next Thursday, we're going deer hunting down there."

So I met him in Mooresville with my old pickup and we headed out. I was usually hunting for brick, and he was usually hunting for deer. I followed him all the way down to the South Carolina line and almost burned up my old truck trying to keep up with him.

I don't remember what type of vehicle he had, but I do remember it had a winch on it. We went to this old house and there was a huge chimney that must have been 40 or 50 feet high. It was that perfect hand-made brick that I had been looking for. The chimney was still standing, and but we really had no way to break it down.

Earnhardt came up with the idea of pulling it down with the winch. The idea was to wrap the cable around it and pull it down with the truck. The cable he had wasn't very long at all, and I told him, "Dale, I don't think you can do that, because if the thing falls in the direction you're pulling it, it's going to land on your vehicle." So he said, "Once I start, I'll just go real fast and outrun it."

Well, I didn't think about it, but my old truck was sitting totally opposite of where the chimney was going to fall. He let the clutch out and the cable sheared right through the chimney and pulled a section of the brick out. But the brick above it twisted and fell across the hood of my truck and dented it in. Luckily, it didn't damage it so bad that I couldn't drive it. He helped me load up all the brick I could hold in that truck and we got back up the road. I told him afterward how much I appreciated the brick, but I didn't want to get any more that way.

So by the end of the day, my truck engine was nearly blown from trying to keep up with Earnhardt, and it was dented up pretty bad from the bricks, but I made it back to Elkin.

There was a time when I rode with him in a race car. The best I remember we were at Rockingham, and he came to me and told me he was going to check the brakes and that was all he was going to do. The track was shut down for lunch. He asked Bill Gazaway, the technical director for NASCAR, if he could take the car out and he said yes. He said to me, "Come on and go with me. I'm not going to go fast because I can't. NASCAR won't let me."

Well, dumb 'ole me just jumped in there with him. He set sail wide open for about three or four laps, and I was holding onto the roll cage sitting right down on the floor. I don't know how fast he ran, but it was fast enough that it got my attention. I owed him one for a long time.

I recall a story that involved Dale and his good friend, the late Tim Richmond. The two were nothing short of fearless on the race track, often making more than one fan or media member catch his breath at the sight of certain crashes or spins.

When Dale went to drive for Bud Moore in 1982, he and Tim used to do some pretty serious racing on the track. They played what people in the sport would call "grab ass," which is bump drafting one another and brake checking one another on the race track. They did that up at Pocono a few times, and Bud was about ready to strangle Earnhardt because he wrecked a car or two up there doing that.

In a race up there in 1982, he did wreck really hard and suffered one of his worst accidents. Earnhardt hit the wall going over the tunnel turn almost head on. It messed his leg up real bad and he suffered a broken kneecap along with some bangs and bruises. The wreck also knocked him unconscious. The track rescue guys took him out of the wreck with the help of a couple of fans from the infield. They got him to the ambulance and took him to the infield care center. They realized he was lapsing in and out of consciousness.

Earnhardt said to me later, "I don't remember hitting the wall, but I do remember thinking that I was going to." They strapped him into a basket-type stretcher that attached to the outside of the helicopter, sort of like what you would see on the old television show, *M.A.S.H.* They would put you in, strap you to the outside and fly you to the hospital. He didn't remember being strapped to a helicopter. When he woke up, the helicopter was taking off en route to the hospital. Dale said, "I realized I had probably hit the wall. I didn't know how bad I was hurt, but I saw I was going up. I was laying down looking at blue sky. My first thought I had was, 'This wreck has taken me out. At least I'm going in the right direction.'"

Dale Earnhardt was a really close friend to me. It's hard to believe he's no longer with us.

32

THE DEER HUNTER

One rather popular hobby among NASCAR drivers is deer hunting. Give drivers a weekend off, the hunting rifle of their choice and a thousand acres, and it's a good bet 12 or 15 people associated with the sport would show up.

Neil Bonnett loved to hunt about as much as he liked to drive race cars. He would go whenever he got the chance, especially if Dale Earnhardt could work it into his schedule to go with him. There were even times Neil found himself killing deer with an unintended weapon, his very own race car.

On the race track at Pocono in the mid-1980s while driving for Junior Johnson, Neil was practicing, and all of a sudden a big one jumped out onto the backstretch and went through the front of his car. There was hair and hooves everywhere with all four legs sticking out of the grille.

Neil nursed his car around the track and came rolling into the garage with this deer splattered all over his windshield. A reporter ran up to the car and asked, "Neil, what in the world happened?"

Neil looked at him, paused solemnly for a moment and said, "Oh GOD, I just killed Bambi!" Neil had a very dry sense of humor and was one of the funniest people I had ever met.

Bobby Allison ran into that same problem once during a practice session, but Harold Kinder, NASCAR's longtime flagman, was having trouble communicating the message to him and had to improvise.

I liked picking on Harold. He was fun to pick on. I would announce over the P.A. stuff like, "There will be a fan club meeting for Harold Kinder in the phone booth on the corner of 5th and Main Street at 4:00 p.m." He'd see me and grin and shake his head or point a finger at me.

Like Neil, Bobby was practicing at Pocono and a deer had been spotted on the backstretch. It was always a danger to have deer come out of the woods there and get on the track.

Obviously, Harold didn't have a flag to indicate that a deer was on the track. So he put a hand up at each ear and put one finger up on each hand as if they were antlers.

Bobby saw Harold as he came by but didn't lift off the throttle. Harold put a finger to each side of his head again on the next lap, but this time Bobby looked up, saw him, and shot him the finger as he passed underneath. The next lap by, the same exchange of gestures happened between them again. Finally, the exchange of signs happened a third time. When Bobby came back around turn four, he missed the deer, but the driver behind him suffered damage to his car. Harold tried to tell him, but Bobby wasn't getting the message.

I laugh openly when he tells the story of Bonnett taking some friends hunting. The outcome of that crazy trip featured a rather incredible outcome.

You never knew when to believe Neil, because you never really knew if he was trying to get something on you. The story I'm about to tell you is true. He swore to me that it was.

Neil said a friend of his in Alabama was a bigger deer hunter than either he or Dale Earnhardt were. And that's saying a lot, because Dale and Neil were both big hunters. Neil said that's all this friend ever wanted to do every spare minute he got.

Neil's friend was always in the woods in a deer stand, and his wife finally got mad at him and threatened to leave him because he would hunt for deer so much and was never home. The wife finally told him, "If you're going to hunt all the time, next time you go, I'm going with you. I'm going to find out what's so exciting about deer hunting." So he called Neil one day and asked him if she could come along and he said she could. So Neil and this guy took the wife out in the woods and taught her how to shoot a rifle.

Neil had access to about 4,000 acres in Alabama on this hunting preserve, so they went out to this vast area to hunt for deer. They put her in the stand and said, "If a deer comes by and you want to shoot it, you know how to do it. We're going down the way over here to another stand." They were serious deer hunters and needed to get away from her.

Neil and his friend had been out in that stand for about 30 minutes and all was pretty quiet. Suddenly, they heard rifle fire from where the woman was. Three shots! *Boom! Boom! Boom!* They got down out of the stand and went to check on her. She was standing there arguing with somebody they didn't know.

She looked hard at the man with her hands on her hips. She said, "That's my deer! I'm certain that's my deer." The man standing there said, "No ma'am, I'm sorry, but that's not your deer." But she said again, "Yes, that's my deer! I shot it! That's my deer. It's mine." The man continued, "No ma'am. That's not your deer."

This conversation went on for about four or five minutes, and Neil and his friend weren't about to get involved. Finally, this guy had had enough of her and said, "Okay, I'll tell you what. You're right. I agree. That's your deer. Just give a minute to get my saddle off of it and you can have it!"

Neil Bonnett swore that was a true story, and I believe it.

33

"GET ME SOME TIRES"

O ne of the key parts of a race car are the tires that are bolted to its spindles. Without rubber meeting the road, the best chassis and the best engines obviously have nowhere to go.

There have been many times tires were the difference between winning and losing.

One incident involved longtime team owner Junie Donlavey of Richmond, Virginia. He and his crew found an ingenious way to stay competitive in one of the early races at Darlington.

Junie Donlavey is one of the most well-liked people in all of NASCAR racing. He fielded a team with a long list of drivers for over 50 years. If you ever wanted to find a gentleman in the garage area, Junie is it.

We were at Darlington one weekend, and I was doing a radio story about tires used there at the track. Darlington is a 1.366-mile speedway that was built in 1950 and the place where many of the great NASCAR stories of all time took place.

Darlington is a gritty and tough old race track with one end slightly wider than the other. That's due to one real important fact; when the track was built by the late Harold Brasington, the man who sold him the land had one stipulation or the whole deal was off. Brasington had to save the minnow pond that was located just outside of what was then turn two. Brasington agreed, but to do that, he had to pull that end of the track in some to dodge the pond, so it wasn't perfectly equal to the other end.

Little did the guy who sold him the land know he had just created two of the toughest first and second turns in all of auto racing. And to this day, teams have to set up their cars for one end and fight like hell to get through the other end. That's one of the things that makes Darlington so special. A lot of racing history has been made there and a lot of people consider it to be hallowed ground.

Well, back to the tires, we had a race at Darlington a few years back and Junie and I sat on pit road wall and talked about those early races at that track. Back in 1950, there wasn't any such thing as a racing tire, other than the hard tires you'd get off of Indy cars. In the inaugural Southern 500 in 1950, tires were popping like popcorn and wouldn't last but just 15 or 20 laps. Junior Johnson once told me he drove a Cadillac in that first race and went through 55 tires before it was over. Johnny Mantz won the race in a black Plymouth using some tires he got from Indianapolis, and they worked because they were so hard.

Like Junior, Junie's driver, Bob Apperson, was also blowing out tires. And Junie was running out.

One of his crew members had an idea. He said, "Why don't we see if we can get the spare tires out of some of the passenger cars in the infield? We'll buy them if they'll sell them to us." So off through the infield they went, searching for a Ford rim and tire that would fit the lug pattern that was on the race car. Some people did sell them, but some said, "No way, I may have a flat on the way home."

The race was still going on and Apperson was still blowing out tires. So Junie and his buddies came across this old Ford truck that was perfect for what they needed. No one was around, so they jacked it up.

They had three tires off when the owner came back and asked, "What in the world are you doing?" They weren't sure if he was going to fight or pull a gun or what he was going to do. Junie explained that they needed the tires for the race and offered to buy the tires. The owner of the truck said, "Hey, I'm a big fan of your driver. You can just have 'em." So they took the tires and the man watched his wheels race on the race track, at least until they blew out.

I recall another story involving Donlavey and his driver, Dick Brooks, in the late 1970s. Dick was involved in a grueling 500-lap race at Dover Delaware.

Dover is a one-mile track that now has a concrete surface, but for a long time it was asphalt. The races there for many years were 500 miles, and it would take forever to complete a race. And needless to say, the drivers were absolutely worn out by the time the checkered flag fell.

Dick was in Junie's car and had been running pretty well. A caution came out, and Dick came to pit road and the crew changed all four tires. A lot of times, Donlavey would save money by buying used tires from Junior Johnson instead of always running new ones.

After the green flag came back out, Brooks got back up to speed but soon discovered he was having a much harder time with his car than before the pit stop. He radioed back to Donlavey in the pits and said, "Junie, this car is all over the place. I can barely hang onto it. The set of tires I have on here now is horrible. I couldn't hold this car in a 40-acre field."

Junie radioed back and said in a calm, deliberate voice, "I don't know what you're complaining about. Cale Yarborough ran them pretty hard up front for the last 100 laps, and they worked just fine for him."

That might have been the one time Brooks was left speechless.

Dick passed away of a heart attack on February 1, 2006. He was a great friend too and losing him really hurts.

34

CALLING PETTY'S 200TH

O f the thousands of races I helped to broadcast, one stands out as the most special of them all. It was the 1984 Pepsi 400 at Daytona International Speedway, the day Richard Petty recorded the 200th victory of his illustrious career on July 4 of that year.

Petty, in the Curb Motorsports Pontiac, won the race in a very close finish against Cale Yarborough, in the Ranier Racing Chevrolet. Petty nipped Yarborough by a few feet at the start-finish line on the final green flag lap to earn the historic victory.

I think what also made that day so special was not only that it was Richard Petty's 200th win but President Ronald Reagan was in attendance. It was the first time in NASCAR history a president of the United States attended a NASCAR event.

I remember that day 22 years ago just as if it were yesterday. The race was so close, I couldn't call it. Mike Joy said, "I think Richard Petty won by inches," and it turned out that he did. It was so close. I was as excited as everybody else when they came off of turn four beating and banging. When they came across the line, I personally didn't think Petty had won from the angle I was looking at it, but it turned out he did.

There was a lot of excitement in the garage area because President Reagan was going to be present. Everybody was speculating, "Will Richard win his 200th race or not?" That pretty much dominated the conversation for the better part of the week down there. The only cat who was pretty laid back about it all was Richard. The press was bugging him all week, and he was as cool as a cucumber.

I felt that Petty was viewed as one of the race favorites. A lot of people believed that if he were going to collect the 200th victory, it would probably happen at Daytona International Speedway, one of his stronger race tracks.

There wasn't any question about that. Everybody knew how hard they had worked to get a car capable of getting his 200th win at Daytona. And Daytona had been his cup of tea for years—he won so many races there. If there was a place he was most likely to get his 200th win, it was Daytona. Everybody felt that way—Richard, his team, and the other drivers.

Petty may have been the favorite, but he didn't win the race very easily. It was right down to the wire. It was not a cut-and-dried situation where he dominated and ran away with the race or had a lap-and-a-half lead. None of us knew who was going to win that race until it was over.

And even though Petty was going for his 200th in front of the president, Yarborough didn't give Petty an inch on the final green-flag lap. The president's presence there didn't make any difference to Cale.

That was one of the most important dates in the history of the sport, and the outcome couldn't have been scripted any better.

For Richard to get that win meant as much to the race fans as having the president there. All in all, I'd say it was one of the milestones that helped NASCAR get to where it is today.

35

HAIL TO
THE CHIEF

Since NASCAR was officially formed in February of 1948, only three presidents have attended events at Daytona International Speedway. I have interviewed presidents Ronald Reagan, George Herbert Walker Bush, and current president, George Walker Bush, during campaign trips and special appearance invitations.

President Jimmy Carter did not attend any NASCAR events during his presidency from 1977 to 1980, but he did once invite NASCAR drivers to a special function at The White House. That particular weekend in the summer of 1977, Carter could not attend due to his involvement in peace talks with Egyptian President Anwar Sadat and Israeli Prime Minister Menachem Begin.

Back when Jimmy Carter was governor of Georgia and running for president in 1976, he attended a race at what was then known as Atlanta International Raceway in the early part of the year. While in Atlanta, he announced in the driver's meeting that if he were elected president he would invite all of the NASCAR drivers to visit him at The White House. I think he was a big race fan at heart and enjoyed hanging around the garage and meeting various drivers and dignitaries during his visits to the race track. He was a very nice person and everyone enjoyed seeing him when he came around.

I also remember an unexpected invitation that occurred during that memorable visit to 1600 Pennsylvania Avenue.

When we went to The White House, it was a very nice event that was hosted by First Lady Rosalynn Carter since the president was at Camp David involved in the peace talks. During the evening I was standing there with David Pearson. We decided to step outside for a while. We were standing in the circular driveway area out front and looked up toward the balcony. There stood Billy Carter, President Carter's brother. He really liked David an awful lot and considered him his favorite driver. Billy had a beer in his hand and he looked down and said, "Hey boys, I'll meet you down at the front door, and I'll show you around this shack!"

Billy would come to the Southern 500 at Darlington when it was held on Labor Day Monday. He would watch some of our all-day Sunday poker games, and we would invite him in. But he would always say, "All you guys are too good for me." Someone would get him in the game and he would clean all of our plows and take everybody's money before the night was over. He was fun to hang out with.

Back at The White House, Billy showed us all around the place, and I could tell the Secret Service agents who were following us around were not real crazy about us being there. They said, "Billy, we really can't let you do this," and Billy would say, "Oh, you all need to back off. These guys are all right. They're my friends."

Billy entered into some restricted areas that he really wasn't supposed to be in. I remember there were red phones all over the place. Finally, the Secret Service put their hands on their guns and said, "That's it. The tour stops right here!"

Pearson piped up and said, "Ok, you're right. It's time to go."

I have to say I enjoyed speaking with all of the presidents who have visited NASCAR races. I remember feeling very much at ease around President Reagan when he came to Daytona in July of 1984. He told

Hall is shown with President George W. Bush and just after the start of the 2004 Daytona 500 at the Daytona International Speedway. Bush was the third sitting president to visit a NASCAR event. *Official White House Photograph/Eric Draper*

me, "I have to be honest with you. I don't know anything about NASCAR other than the fact they go around in a circle. But it really looks exciting."

To me, President Reagan seemed so genuine and down to earth. He was a very nice person, and I really liked him a lot.

One of the funniest but slightly embarrassing stories involved President Bush during his visit to the MRN booth during the 2004 Daytona 500. He was at the track that day and we knew he was coming by, but he came in much earlier than expected. I thought he was going to stay maybe a minute or two, but he decided to stay quite a bit longer.

The NASCAR flagman was getting ready to drop the green flag over the Daytona 500, and the drivers were getting ready to go. Seeing we were ready to start the race, I asked him if he would like to start the Daytona 500, and he said, "Yeah."

I started to say what I usually say to those who call the start, which is basically, "Here they come, and there they go." But I'm glad I didn't say that. I just told him to essentially say that they were coming to the green flag for the start, and that's exactly what he said.

He was to stay a lap or two but he stayed for the first four or five laps. I said to him, "I'm sure you have other dignitaries to visit with, Mr. President, and thank you for stopping by." We said our goodbyes, and he thanked us for allowing him to drop by and then we went to a commercial.

Well, President Bush still had his headset on. We had Dave Moody stationed over in turn one and someone asked Dave off the air amongst ourselves what he thought about Bush's start of the race. Dave says, "Well, I'll tell you one thing. He ain't no Barney Hall." I was about to fall through the floor because I knew the president still had his headset on. President Bush looked at me and smiled and said, "You tell 'em they're right!" And we shook hands and off he went. I don't believe I'll ever forget that as long as I live.

36

TIM AND HARRY

O ne of the most storied combinations between driver and crew
chief in NASCAR Winston Cup competition came with the
late Tim Richmond and his crew chief, the late Harry Hyde.
To say their working relationship started off being mismatched was a
true understatement. Eventually, they would enjoy great success for
two seasons together in a very short period of time.

When Tim and Harry got together at Hendrick Motorsports at the
beginning of the 1986 season, they were about as compatible as oil
and water. The two came from different eras with different beliefs,
especially when it came to race cars and how to drive them.

Tim first joined NASCAR in 1980 and enjoyed a dramatic rise to
the top. He won rookie honors in 1981, won two races in '82 three
more from 1983 through 1985, and seven for Hendrick Motorsports
in 1986. His striking good looks could have landed him a male
modeling or acting job, and I think he did some of that. And his
charisma could attract the biggest of sponsors, simply by selling them
his charm and flamboyant, outgoing personality.

Tim knew no other way to drive but flat out, and if he burned the tires off the car or took the car to the garage early because he had blown the motor or ripped out the transmission, so be it. That was racing, and if Richmond didn't win, he bitterly accepted his loss.

Harry was a crusty old crew chief who was older than dirt. He had seen every hot shot driver come through the gate and every trick in the book when it came to building race cars. Hyde won the NASCAR championship with Bobby Isaac in 1970 and won a great many races with other drivers such as Bobby Allison, Dave Marcis, Neil Bonnett, Geoff Bodine, Cale Yarborough, Buddy Baker, and Richmond.

Harry was a smart crew chief who knew it all and had seen it all. He tried and tried to get Tim to listen to him about being there at the end and how to save his equipment, and once Tim started listening, they started winning.

Tim was an exceptional talent behind the wheel. He could do anything with a car, even drive it in reverse the length of pit road and pit backward with a bad transmission and still win. He did that at Pocono in '86, and Pocono was one of his magic tracks. He became sick with what they thought was pneumonia in the winter months just before the start of the 1987 season. He sat out for a good portion of the season and came back in June to win back-to-back races there at Pocono and on the road course at Riverside, California.

Tim drove in the next six races but never won again. At Michigan in August, some of the drivers were complaining to NASCAR about his erratic driving on the track. He also seemed to be so out of sorts just before it was time for him to qualify there. He left Hendrick Motorsports a few days after that race, and the truth concerning his illness would eventually surface over the next year. He attempted a comeback for the 1988 Daytona 500, but NASCAR wouldn't let him drive and that was pretty much the end of his career. Tim died of AIDS on August 13, 1989. Had he lived, I feel sure he would have been a NASCAR champion several times over, I really do. He was just starting to show what tremendous talent he really had before his career was unexpectedly cut short.

Harry could do a hundred things to a race car, but one thing he would do was something similar to what is done today with spring rubbers to tighten them up. Back then you wanted the spring to sit up so high, especially in qualifying. You had to have a way to keep the car about six or eight inches from the bottom of the bumper to the race track. Nowadays, it's two inches or even an inch in some cases.

When Bobby Allison drove the K and K Dodge in 1967, Harry figured out a way to put some wooden blocks in the springs of the car. They would take two laps to qualify, and Bobby would go out and build up a little bit of speed. As he went down the straightaway, Bobby would find a way to make the car bump, even if he had to drive down to the bottom to make it do it. When he did, the weight of the car would crush the blocks and they would fall out. Then the car would drop when the spring compressed. The car became lower and would glide through the air and obviously go faster. They won a lot of pole positions doing that. He was a master at going fast. His cars won 56 races and over $4 million in winnings with Harry.

Harry was a good guy. We lost him to a heart attack in 1996. When I first got into racing, Harry knew who I was and knew I had been doing radio. He came over to me one day and said, "Hall, I'm going to tell you something. I know you need to get the inside scoop on what's going on in racing so you'll have something to talk about on the radio." He said, "I'm going to tell you how to do that. The easiest way to find out anything that's going on in racing is to go in the restroom in the garage, get in one of those stalls early in the morning, put your feet up on the seat so nobody knows you're there and just sit there for about 30 minutes. At a given point, every son-of-a-gun in the business will come in that restroom and they'll talk about what's going on. And you'll know every damn thing in racing!" And he was pretty close to right. I tried it a time or two and it worked.

I remember a funny incident that may serve as the one time someone got Harry's goat. Or in this case, Harry's fish.

There was a time when Harry went fishing and caught a pretty good-sized catfish. Harry caught this fish out of Lake Norman, which is where a lot of drivers have their homes in North Carolina. Well, he put this fish in a five-gallon bucket and took him back and put him in this pond that was behind the shop. It was just a small pond and it wasn't all that big. Well, for some reason, Harry decided to keep that fish and not cook him. So he put him in his pond and he kept him out there for several months and kept feeding him bread and treated him like his pet fish. Over time, Harry got the fish to come and eat off the top of the water. Harry was really proud of that catfish.

The thing was he didn't tell anybody about it.

Well, Harry went to Daytona for a test session. He came back a day or two later and he went out to feed his fish, but he wouldn't come up to the top of the water. The next day, Harry went back out to feed him and, again, he didn't come to the top of the water. He was wondering what the devil was going on.

One of the guys in the shop saw him throwing that food in the water and he walked over to Harry and said, "Harry, what in the world are you trying to feed in there?" Harry said, "I've got a pretty good-sized catfish out here I caught in Lake Norman a while back." This guy says, "Oh, Lord. We were out here the other day and someone said they saw the water roll up. One of the guys said he thought there were fish out there, so one of the guys went and got a rod and reel and caught that fish. What's worse is we dressed it and had him for lunch the other day when you went to test. We made catfish stew with him."

Harry walked off and didn't speak to the crew for a week after that, not even about the race car. Harry was quite a character.

When team owner Rick Hendrick put Tim and Harry together, Hyde told him he wasn't interested in, "raisin' anymore younguns." But the two did reluctantly join forces, and like Harry predicted, had a rather turbulent yet strangely respectful relationship with one another.

Tim and I were pretty close. He was always calling me "NASCAR Stooge." Richmond would always criticize NASCAR for everything they did. I would sometimes try to explain why they would do things the way they did, and we would have some friendly arguments over certain issues. He said I was always on NASCAR's side on everything, so he gave me the nickname.

I knew Tim and Harry very well and often spent time with them in the garage area. One particular day I observed one of the best definitions of their friendship in action.

We were in Pocono and I was supposed to ride back to the hotel with some of the Motor Racing Network guys. They thought I went back with someone else, so they left me there. So I found that I didn't have a way back to the hotel. Harry asked me if I had a ride, and I told him those cats had taken off and left me. He said, "Come on. You can ride with me and Tim."

A lot of people may not know this, but Harry and Tim fussed at each other all the time. They were at each other's throats night and day, even with all the success they had together. They never agreed on anything.

From the minute we got in the car, Tim and Harry had been arguing about qualifying that day. Tim won the pole for the race, but he was on Harry's case about the springs and shocks in the car. Tim kept telling him all the things that were wrong with the car and how his ideas didn't work. They were having a pretty hot argument about who was right and who was wrong.

So we were riding to the hotel and Tim was driving, Harry was up front, and I was riding in the back seat. Once we got out in front of the race track, Tim, like most race drivers in those days, was running 80 miles per hour down a 55 mile-per-hour highway. Harry said to Tim, "Boy, you'd better slow down. You're gonna get a ticket." Tim just rolled his eyes over at Harry and stayed on the gas.

Harry hadn't gotten his warning out of his mouth before Tim looked up and saw a blue light in his rearview mirror. About that time we heard the siren and saw the lights, and sure enough, here came a Pennsylvania state trooper after Tim. He pulled us over.

So when the cop came up, he looked at Tim and said, "Young man, do you realize you were running 80 in a 55 zone?" Tim said, "No, I was not aware of that." The patrolman said, "Well, according to my radar, you were." Tim said, "I don't care what your radar said. I wasn't running that speed, was I, Harry?"

Harry leaned over and said, "Officer, if I was you I would never argue with him when he's been drinking!"

The cop didn't think it was funny at all. He asked Richmond to step outside the car. He made him walk the line and touch his nose, and Harry was sitting on the hood of the car laughing his rear end off. The cop finally came over to Harry and said, "I don't appreciate your sense of humor. I take speeding very seriously. I'm going to give you a break this time, but don't let me catch you running like this again."

Tim got his warning ticket and slowly moved back on the highway. They weren't on the road 10 seconds before Harry and Tim started arguing again. And they continued arguing all the way back to the hotel.

I should say they argued at least during the times when Harry wasn't laughing about the deal with the cop. Harry loved to get anything on Tim, and he got a real kick out of that.

Individually, Tim and Harry were two of the very best in the business. Together, they were simply magic.

37

JUMP IN AND TAKE OFF

No matter how well things are planned and scheduled minute to minute during a race weekend, the unexpected will happen from time to time.

On July 27, 1986, Talladega Superspeedway definitely experienced the unexpected. As a result, some policies pertaining to prerace activities were changed that continue to exist today.

I was standing in the radio booth with my headset in place just minutes away from going live. A commotion erupted on pit road that took everyone by surprise.

I was there at Talladega that day in the booth, but we hadn't gone on the air yet. There was a public relations person who worked for NASCAR who had driven a pace car out on the frontstretch to take the Grand Marshall of the race to the prerace stage so he could give the command to start the race. This official was doing the right thing by leaving the door open and the car's air conditioning running, because it gets so hot at Talladega. He parked it there on the front stretch and got out to help get the Grand Marshall to his position. They were just about to give the command to fire the engines, and all of the sudden this guy came out of nowhere, jumped in the pace car, popped it in gear and took off. The tower thought it was a track official, but after a quick count of noses, they discovered it wasn't one of them.

Now, it was so close to race time that the television networks had already come on the air. Needless to say, they had their cameras trained on this bright red pace car, and this guy was hauling the mail in it toward turn one.

I can't remember if he made a full lap or if they immediately took off behind him, but he was soon joined by two motorcycle cops, the Alabama State Police, the County Sheriff, some safety trucks and a track official or two. I'm sure he saw all of these law officers coming for him with their lights flashing in the rearview mirror, but he just stayed on the throttle. Some estimated he was doing over a hundred miles an hour all the way around.

Truthfully, I really didn't know what was going on at first. Most of the fans didn't have scanners back then and they didn't know, either. I think some people thought it was a stunt. A few crew guys on pit road were way out in the grass cheering him on. Tim Brewer was laughing so hard he could barely catch his breath.

The guy came back around after making one full lap and three-fourths of another lap, and it's a wonder he didn't run over somebody. He got to turn four and found track officials had positioned three wrecker trucks across the turn to stop him. He came through there pretty fast and he was lucky he didn't wreck the car and kill himself. Driving on a high-banked turn at a high rate of speed is tricky if you've never done it. He could have torn that car all to pieces.

For a split second, he was going to go for it and was going to crash his way through the trucks. But he slid to a stop sideways and left some skid marks behind him. The security guys and police jumped in there and wrestled him out of the car and took him off to jail. All he wanted was his moment in the sun, and I guess he got it.

The thing was he had to go through the tunnel and get through quite a few fences to get to that part of the track. I heard he hid in a van to get through a tunnel to the infield, but how he got through or around all those fences without getting caught, I don't know. He didn't have a race ticket in his possession.

I heard he came from Lincoln, Alabama, just down the way on a motorcycle he was test driving before buying it. He blended into race traffic, ditched the bike once he got on track property and later hid in the van to get past the ticket takers. Sadly, there were certainly some issues going on with him that needed to be addressed.

I never heard anybody say exactly why he decided to take to the high banks of Talladega that day. Whatever the reason was, something just possessed him to jump in that pace car and take off.

38

TRAGEDY AT RICHMOND

S unday, February 25, 1990 ranks as probably the coldest race day
NASCAR has ever faced. It came in the second race of the
season at Richmond International Raceway as an unusual burst
of cold air that blanketed the Notheastern United States. Anyone who
was outside had to put on layer after layer of clothing. By 1 p.m. the
high temperature was recorded at only five degrees. It was so cold it
hurt to breathe. It's a day that's still talked about in the garage area
today.

By nightfall, it would also become the day I suffered one of the
worst accidents of my life.

I still get cold thinking about that day at Richmond. Bitter is about
the only word good enough to describe how cold it was. The sun
shined all day, but it didn't help very much. It was just too cold to
enjoy a race of any kind, and I felt for the fans up on those cold metal
bleachers. I was at least in the booth and had heat and wasn't out in
it. I have to admit I felt bad for every other soul in racing down on pit
road having to endure the raw conditions, including all of my MRN
colleagues. About the warmest people out around the track were those

who were driving the race cars. It was one time when those header pipes that ran under the floorboard and under their seats were great to have since they pumped heat into the cockpits of the race cars. I'll bet they really felt good.

That day, Mark Martin won the race but was found to have an illegal carburetor spacer on his engine. NASCAR let the win stand, but Mark and team owner Jack Roush were fined $40,000 and docked 46 championship points. As season's end, Martin finished second to Dale Earnhardt and team owner Richard Childress in their bid for the championship. The margin between Earnhardt and Martin was 26 points, and had Mark not lost those points at Richmond, it may have made a difference in the outcome.

I was already leaving the track when the writers began reworking their stories due to the late word of Martin's postrace inspection problems. As it turned out, I was wishing I was back up there with them. If I had, I wouldn't have been hit, along with MRN announcer Jim Phillips, by a motor home on the street in front of the speedway.

Laburnum Avenue is a four-lane road with a median in the center. We got across the first two lanes, stopped and looked to the left. We stepped out and had no idea the motor home was coming. It seemed like it came out from nowhere. We just didn't see him. I still don't know where he came from. We both suffered some broken bones and spent a couple of months recuperating and being sore.

A few hours after being admitted to the hospital, I remember one strange phone call that came into the hospital switchboard that night. I was lying in my hospital bed with three broken ribs. I was in a lot of pain and on some pretty strong pain medicine.

The door to my room opened and the nurse came in and asked if I felt up to taking a phone call. I said I was okay enough for that, and they patched the call into my room. It was a voice I didn't recognize. "You okay?" the person asked. I said, "Yeah, I guess I am." The person on the other end said, "Are ya sure you're okay?" Then he started laughing, and I knew who it was. "Is this Earnhardt?" I asked. He said, "Yeah, but let me ask you a question. How in the hell can you sit up there in that booth every Sunday and call all those races if you're so blind you can't see something as big as a motor home?" All I could say was, "Well, somehow I've made my way through, I guess."

We continued to talk and before the conversation ended, he offered to fly my mother up to Richmond to be with me. I was quite appreciative of the offer, but since I was scheduled to go home in a day or two, I declined.

I was told later that an announcement was made in the press box and media center that we had been hurt pretty badly. I hate to say it, but I remember that terrible day very well. I received a lot of nice cards and notes during my recovery period, and I really appreciated all of them. That's one thing about the NASCAR community; when a person is in need, everyone seems to come running.

There was a pretty funny joke played on Jim and me the next spring when the tour came to Richmond on a return visit. This was a year later, and Tim Brewer was working as Junior Johnson's crew chief. We were back at Richmond, and Brewer came over and asked us what we were doing for lunch. I told him we would be around the garage. He told us that Junior was planning to hold a press conference at noon and we might need to bring a tape recorder.

We got there about five or 10 minutes before noon, and there were plenty of media people there but also crew people as well. I didn't think anything about it. So Jim and I went bopping up there and Brewer stepped out of the truck. I said, "Where's Junior?" Brewer said, "He's in the front of the truck. But we've got something for you guys."

Brewer went back into the truck and brought out a cake that was four feet by four feet. There was a little model of a motor home and there were two little plastic figures lying in the icing of the cake. The cake read, "Happy Anniversary You Dumb Butts!"

I still owe Brewer for that one.

39

WALLY THE THIEF

T ape recorders have always been a tremendous tool for any journalist who covers the NASCAR Nextel Cup circuit. Quotes are taken and transcribed or played on MRN broadcasts.

There was one time in 1996 when I was very glad that I listened to my tape before playing it over the airwaves.

We were at Charlotte one weekend and I needed to do an interview with Wally Dallenbach when he was driving for Bud Moore. Bud had been around since 1961 and worked as a mechanic before he started fielding his own cars. He had drivers like Fireball Roberts, Joe Weatherly, Bob Welborn, Pearson, Darel Dieringer, Lee Roy Yarbrough, Buddy Baker, Isaac, the list was a long one. All told, he won 63 races with his last win coming in 1993 with Geoffrey Bodine. The last time he fielded a car was for Ted Musgrave in 2000.

If you looked up the word "Ford," you'd most likely see his picture there. His and the Wood Brothers. That's all they've ever run for the past 50 years. Bud was also pretty big into Trans Am Racing for a few years in the late 1960s.

I was talking with Wally when Bud came in the transporter and said, "Come here, Barney. I need to tell you about something real quick." So I put the tape recorder down on the sofa they had up in the little room at the front of the transporter. It was a lounge but also a place Bud used for his office when he was at the track.

I talked to Bud for about four or five minutes and then I finally went and sat down. I asked Wally one more question on tape and then went back to the MRN truck. I was transferring some of those recordings I had gathered through the day over to a master tape to play in our broadcast the next day. I was sitting there listening, and suddenly, there was a strange voice on the tape and it caught me off guard. It was a voice I didn't recognize, but it was like he was interviewing me. He was asking questions like, "Do you still beat your wife?" and "Do you still like to date men?" "You wouldn't believe what Barney Hall does to little animals!" Stuff like that. I thought, "What in the devil is this?" I knew I hadn't put anything like that on there myself. Finally, I figured out the voice was Wally. He had taken my tape recorder and recorded that mess on there when Bud called me out to talk.

I found Wally a little later in the garage, and he was laughing when he saw me walk up. I told him, "Boy, it's a good thing I didn't put all that crap right out on the air." He said, "I didn't figure you would."

The guys in the garage have really liked to pick on me over the years. And unfortunately, I've fallen for an awful lot of it.

40

DALE FINALLY WINS THE 500

When one says the name Dale Earnhardt, another name usually comes to mind; the Daytona International Speedway. For two decades, Earnhardt dominated victory lane at Daytona in the Pepsi 400 NASCAR Winston Cup events, NASCAR Busch Series competition, 125-mile qualifying events, and IROC (International Race of Champions) events. He had won 32 races at Daytona prior to the 1998 Daytona 500 (and 34 total through 2000), more than any other driver in its history. Year after year, he kept missing the biggest jewel—the Daytona 500.

In 19 attempts from 1979 through 1997, Earnhardt seemingly couldn't buy that win, coming close but losing the race in the closing laps due to cut tires, running out of fuel, and being passed by fellow competitors. It looked as if Earnhardt would never get a Daytona 500 victory.

I remember that magic day when Earnhardt finally scored that elusive Daytona 500 victory. It was Sunday, February 15, 1998, the day Earnhardt enjoyed the greatest of his 76 career victories.

Earnhardt had been trying to win that race for 20 years and just couldn't find that last little bit he needed to get it done. That is, until 1998, when he raced back to the caution flag and white flag with a couple of laps to go. Once the caution came out, he made it back to the start-finish line. There weren't enough laps left to get the race back under green.

Over the years, we had traveled together quite a bit and were very close friends. I knew just how bad he wanted to win that race. That was what he talked about most. I saw him get really frustrated after a lot of those 500s. Dale Jr. even said he was hard to live with for a few weeks after that race and usually didn't get back to being himself again until about the middle of March. Losing that race really ate at him. He wanted it real bad.

That day, I kept expecting something to happen on that white-flag lap, just like some of the crazy things that had happened to him in the past. There were times when he cut a tire or ran out of gas or got passed with a couple of laps to go. He would come so close to winning it. But this time he came across the line under the checkered flag, and I admit I was pretty choked up about calling that finish.

I had seen him run that race and almost not want to because he was so tired of having to explain why he hadn't won it. But not on that day. It was finally his.

When we finally got off the air, I went down to victory lane and met him. When he saw me walk into victory lane, he stuck his finger out and pointed to me and then ran over and gave me a hug. He said, "Hey, you old geezer, I finally did it!" And I said, "Yeah, you did!"

It was about the only time I ever saw a couple of tears in the boy's eyes. That day, he could hardly talk to the media or anybody else because the excitement of finally winning the race was overwhelming. About a half hour after the race, I think it finally soaked in. I don't think there was anyone there who wasn't emotionally choked up that day. It meant an awful lot to me and so many others to see him do it.

I think one of the most touching moments of that day was every crew member and every team owner in the garage area came out to pit road to shake his hand as he drove to victory lane. There was a long line of colored uniforms all the way down pit road—people just wanted to shake his hand. That was quite impressive to see him receive congratulations from all of them. He finally couldn't contain his excitement any longer and started doing doughnuts all around the infield grass before he pulled into victory lane.

It was one of the happiest days I ever spent at a race track.

41

SAD SUNDAYS AND OTHER BAD DAYS

Sundays around NASCAR Nextel Cup tracks are usually filled with the glory of winning, and once per season, the celebration of a championship and the crowning of a champion.

Then, on the other end of the spectrum are those rare days when drivers lose their lives at the controls of their race cars.

Unfortunately, there have been sad days in this business. Up until about 10 years ago, we were all a lot closer to the drivers than we are now. The guys who have begun racing in the past seven or eight years you know on a first-name basis and you're friends with them, but it's not really like it was before. We used to stay at the same hotels as the drivers and go out to eat together, but that's not done as much now as it used to be. Those days are long gone.

It's always really hard to have to pass along tragic news.

I've been in the booth for many of those sad Sundays when tragedy overshadowed the storyline of the day. There's just no easy way to deal with the loss of a driver, especially for those who are professionally associated with the sport. Drivers, team owners, crew members, and media alike know them personally and become close friends over a long period of time.

NASCAR, as well as many companies associated with the sport, have spent countless hours working on safety for the drivers, crew members and the fans. That's the absolute number-one item on NASCAR's agenda above anything else. Fast speeds, however, can generate some outcomes we simply hate to see happen. When it's a person's time to go, no amount of safety can change that outcome.

A crash that didn't appear to be serious was suffered by Larry Smith at Talladega, Alabama, on August 12, 1973. Smith's brush with the wall seemed so light that many in the garage thought he would quickly return to action. His crew chief was working on the car in hopes of getting back in the race when he was shocked to learn that Smith had not survived.

If you were to look at the accident on tape today, you would still say that accident couldn't have hurt anybody. He literally just grazed the wall. It would be like driving down the interstate and momentarily taking your eyes off the road and the car you're driving hits the guardrail and just bounces right back into the highway and you keep on going. He brushed the wall just a little bit on the passenger side and was running toward the back of the field at the time of the accident. He stayed up on that wall for 10 or 15 seconds and everyone went by, and then the car turned and went right down to the apron and stopped. It looked like he had kept the car up on the wall to keep it out of the way and then parked it. The report on the accident said it was believed that he died the minute he hit the wall.

I was there helping to announce the Talladega 500 on August 10, 1975, when Dewayne "Tiny" Lund, 42, lost his life in an accident in the early stages of the race. Tiny's biggest NASCAR victory came when he won the 1963 Daytona 500 as a relief driver for Marvin Panch who had been burned in a sports car crash.

The crash that took Lund's life was one of those wrecks where he was hit in the driver's side door by another driver who was going pretty fast. I remember Ken Squier said, "Ladies and gentlemen, it's my sad duty to pass this news along to you that Tiny Lund lost his life in a crash here at Talladega earlier today." Those are always hard words for anyone to convey, whether speaking one on one or to an audience a million strong.

I knew Tiny but not real well. I knew that you didn't want to make him mad and that he had a wild sense of humor and was subject to do anything in the world at any time.

I recall another tragic accident that occurred at Talladega Superspeedway, then known as Talladega International Motor Speedway on May 5, 1974. A wet pit road from rain mixed with oil from a blown engine made it icy slick. The accident occurred during a caution period on the 105th lap of the 188-lap race.

I was working turn four that day at Talladega and believe it or not was positioned on top of a restroom as my vantage point. I saw the car Grant Adcox was driving get out of control, and he slammed into the pit road wall rather hard. Don Miller, (current president of Penske Racing South) was working as catch can man that day for Penske Racing and driver Gary Bettenhausen. I remember seeing him get pinned between the car and the pit road wall, but I never did see him after that. I believe it knocked him completely under the car. Don lost his leg in that accident and has had difficulties from the accident for many years. Buddy Parrott, a longtime NASCAR crew chief, took off his belt and put it around Don's leg and made a tourniquet and cut off the blood flow. Had he not done that, Don would have bled to death.

Grant came off the banking and hit pit road, and I remember he was way out toward the grass, and I think he may have gotten two wheels out in it and just lost control and spun around backward down pit road. Grant was an easygoing sort who raced in ARCA for years and appeared in some NASCAR Winston Cup events. Grant died in a single-car accident at Atlanta during the last NASCAR Winston Cup race of the 1989 season on November 19 of that year.

Another of my close friends was lost on August 11, 1991. His name was John Delpus "J.D." McDuffie, an independent driver who didn't receive factory support from the Detroit automakers. McDuffie carried sponsorship from Tom Rumple and Rumple Furniture, a local business there in Elkin.

J.D. was someone I thought an awful lot of. It was very difficult to finish the race broadcast the day J.D. was killed at Watkins Glen, New York. He and I played a lot of poker together. If there was a poker game going, he was in it. J.D. was just a wonderful person. He was one of those people you honestly couldn't find a bad thing to say about. He had a small team that he fielded himself. There are only about two or three people in this business who you could never say anything bad about, and he was one of them. The day he died was a very sad day for racing.

J.D. ran off the road course and his car flipped and landed upside down. Apparently the car hit a support post and it penetrated through the top of the car and caused him to suffer a severe head injury. He was only 52 years old.

J.D. was such a good person. I really miss him and think of him often.

On April 1, 1993, NASCAR's reigning champion, Alan Kulwicki, died in an airplane crash as his pilots attempted to land at the Bristol airport in Bristol, Tennessee. Less than five months after being crowned the 1992 NASCAR Winston Cup champion, he was gone at 38 years old.

I was in my hotel room in Bristol the night Alan died when someone called and told me to turn on my television. They said they thought Alan and some of his guys were on the airplane, but didn't know for sure. Soon after, the news said everyone on board the plane had been lost.

The next day was probably the weirdest day I had ever spent at a race track. When I got to the track the next morning, Alan's transport rig was leaving, and all of the team members were standing at attention with their hats over their hearts. Peter Jellen was Alan's truck driver then, and he made a lap around the Bristol Motor Speedway and went out of the track. That day, you could have heard a pin drop all day long. There was no life in the garage area to speak of. The guys on the crews went about their business, but they were only going through the motions. Everyone was saying this would have been what he wanted, for us to continue on and keep racing. That was a very, very strange day.

I got to know Alan Kulwicki pretty well about two years before he won his championship in 1992. Junior Johnson wanted to hire him, and I was kind of the unofficial intermediary between the two at the time. I got to know quite a bit about Alan. He was an independent soul, I can tell you that. He was a hard man to deal with. In essence, he didn't want to drive for anybody else. He said he had had several offers already, and he just wanted to do his own thing because he thought he could do it. And he proved to be right.

Alan was all business. I would see him in a bar, and he would mingle socially with his crew, but he wasn't a real outgoing person. He was really hard to get to know. But for the most part, my impression of him was that he was strictly business about racing. He was dead serious about it. And he was going to make darn sure that he was a success at it.

On July 13, 1993, NASCAR superstar Davey Allison died from injuries suffered in a private helicopter crash the previous day at Talladega Superspeedway.

I watched Davey Allison grow up. I got to know him more by talking about airplanes than race cars. His dad, Bobby Allison, was into flying pretty heavy, and Davey was also learning to fly. He probably could have gotten a ride in a Cup car maybe two years earlier than he did, but Bobby didn't want him to enter Cup racing until he was absolutely ready to. Bobby made darn sure that Davey knew every working piece of a race car. I think that's why from the time he stepped into a so so car, he would give it a better ride than most guys could. Bobby made him learn everything about a race car so that if something wasn't working, he would know what to do to fix it.

Davey wanted to enter Cup racing really badly in the mid-1980s. But Bobby told him he wasn't ready, and he stayed at the shop and built cars and toughed it out. And if his grades suffered, Bobby and wife Judy would put the clamps on his short track racing.

I liked Davey an awful lot. He was friendly and very outgoing. I never heard him say a bad word about anybody the whole time I knew him.

The helicopter crash that he suffered will always be a great mystery, I guess. Someone at MRN called me at home and told me about the crash. I tried several times to reach Bobby on the phone but wasn't able to. I'm sure half the people in racing were trying to get him. I did get to talk with someone at the hospital in racing, and they filled me in on how bad the situation was. They told me it was pretty bad and that he probably wouldn't make it through the night. He died at seven o'clock the next morning. That was another tough day to have to go through, both for Davey's family and everyone in the sport. Davey was very well liked in this business and would have gone far had he lived.

The only spin I can put on it that makes any sense is that it was just his time to leave here. He was going to land in one place there at Talladega and then at the last second, decided to move over a couple hundred feet and that was the difference between living and dying as it turned out. There was really no explanation for it. I don't think Red Farmer, the close friend he was flying with that day, or Neil Bonnett or Bobby or anybody else had an explanation.

Neil was a friend and a broadcast colleague. Bonnett honed his craft and became very good as a television announcer. He died after a crash during practice at Daytona on February 11, 1994.

Neil was one of the nicest people in this business. He was one heck of a good driver, but he was also a heck of a friend. He was that way to hundreds of people in this business.

If Neil were still around today, he would be in trouble all of the time because he spoke his mind and told you what he thought about another driver or something NASCAR did that he didn't think was right, or whatever.

On the track, Neil was as competitive as Dale Earnhardt and had some rather fierce, knock-down, drag-out battles with him on the race track. Neil was another driver who had a heart of gold. People talk about the guys who will always give you a good interview and are easy to talk to, and Neil was one of them. Neil would never turn anybody down, whether you were TV, radio, or a small-town newspaper. He would listen to what you said, and he was one of the few guys in that era who would. He would try really hard to give you a good answer every time.

I remember how talented Bonnett was in front of the camera. He was very knowledgeable about the sport and could convey his thoughts smoothly and easily. Fans loved him because they could understand him. Ironically, Bonnett never felt he was very good at it.

Sadly, Neil returned to the cockpit to drive one more limited schedule and lost his life before he took the green flag.

A major TV network was talking with him about joining them, and he asked me if I thought he could do it. I said, "Sure, I think you can." He said, "I'm a country boy and I have an accent, and they aren't gonna want me." I said, "Listen, I found out a long time ago that in this business you shouldn't change anything. Just be Neil Bonnett. If that works that's fine, and if it doesn't then you don't need to do it." That's exactly what he did. He was as down to earth and as natural as anyone I've ever seen, just as if we were sitting in his living room talking. He eventually did go to work in television and did a great job as a commentator.

He was the same with the press. One writer approached Neil about writing a book about his life, and he was shocked. Neil said, "Why in the world would anyone want to read a story about me?" And he was dead serious. Neil was just a very humble guy, even when he was on top of his game. When I got word that Neil had died, I was just numb and stayed that way for several days.

There have been other crashes over the years that were quite severe. I've seen a lot of wrecks that really scared me. When Bobby Allison got hurt so bad at Pocono in June of 1988, I thought he might not make it. I was a bundle of nerves all day long after Bobby's crash.

Bobby was trying to make it back to the pits to replace a flat rear tire when he spun up toward the wall. He was there a few seconds sitting still, and another driver came through there at a high rate of speed and hit him in the driver's side door.

Alan Bestwick was working the area where he crashed that day and he came to me off the air and told me things really didn't look good for Bobby. Alan also told me Bobby had taken a really hard hit. I remember we kept checking back with Alan while they were working to get Bobby out. I also remember that Davey Allison (Bobby's son) would stop his race car at that location, trying to get any information he could on his Dad's condition. He probably stopped six or eight times.

Dick Brooks had retired from driving and was helping us with the broadcast. He was down there when they brought him into the infield care center. He told us off the air that Bobby was hurt really bad. I couldn't get that out of my mind that day. Bobby and I were, at times, the best of friends and other times, we were really digging at each other. But I respected Bobby as much as anybody in the business.

Allison did eventually recover from those injuries, but it took years for him to get back to good health. Had the crash at Pocono not happened, Bobby might be driving today. I feel like there would be a good chance he would be driving something, a NASCAR Craftsman Truck Series truck, or like Pearson, something on a local short track.

There have been some wrecks that have looked mighty spectacular, but the fact that the car is rolling and tumbling around in the air is really the best kind of wreck to have to experience. It's the ones where a driver takes a hard head-on hit, like Earnhardt, or being hit in the driver's door, like Bobby, that can be really bad. They are more dangerous because you're being hit so quickly. The ones that have hurt people or cost them their lives are when they run head on into the wall or T-boned another car. Other wrecks with spectacular flips that come to mind involve Ryan Newman at Daytona and Elliott Sadler at Talladega. Those two both walked away.

We saw Richard Petty's wreck when he got airborne in the Daytona 500 in 1988. And we saw the same sort of thing happen with Rusty Wallace in 1991 when he was tapped by Earnhardt at Talladega. I don't think NASCAR has really had anyone get hurt real bad in those end-over-end-type wrecks.

I remember Darrell Waltrip got hit in the driver's side door at Daytona in the early 1990s and broke his leg. About four or five years later, he rolled a car pretty violently at Daytona and had some scrapes and bruises but wasn't seriously injured.

Then there was the crash that Michael Waltrip had during a NASCAR Busch race in 1990. He hit a crossover gate and the car just went up in a thousand pieces. But somehow he wasn't hurt. The motor was one way, and the rest of the car was broken up in several pieces. But there he sat, still in his seat, and he just stood up and walked away. I was certain that boy was dead. There was no way he couldn't be. But we've seen a dozen crashes over the years where drivers definitely had someone riding with them. That's for sure.

Both Adam Petty, 20, and Kenny Irwin, 30, lost their lives in crashes during practice sessions at New Hampshire International Speedway on May 12, 2000 and July 7, 2000, respectively.

I got to know Adam the last year he raced before he died. He loved to talk into a microphone and loved being on both radio and TV and any public appearances he could do. He loved to talk about racing. That's all that he wanted to talk about. I learned in the little bit of time I spent with him what his Dad, Kyle Petty, meant to him.

Kyle was the man who got him straightened out. Not that he was a wild child or anything like that. I don't think he was that motivated in the beginning when he drove an old NASCAR Busch Series car, in my opinion. I think somewhere in all of that, Adam and Kyle sat down, and his daddy said, "Look, either you're going to be a race driver or you're just going work around the shop and not take this thing seriously." I think he probably took his dad's advice to heart. Or he took someone's advice to heart, whether it was Richard or Dale Inman or maybe a combination of the three that got him to thinking,

"Hey, I'm a Petty and I want to be a race car driver." He was a good one, and his death, too, was a hard loss.

I never got to know Kenny Irwin that well. I interviewed him maybe a half-dozen times, and he seemed to be a warm, caring human being. But he was pretty motivated and determined. I think that boy had pressure on him from the day he stepped into Robert Yates's car. There was a ton of pressure on that boy. He put a lot of pressure on himself to succeed. He didn't have much time to get to know people, because he was too busy trying to figure out that race car and trying to get a decent chemistry going with the people he worked with.

Just about the time he was about to get things turned around and there was a good chemistry forming after he'd moved to another team, he lost his life.

One of my closest relationships in racing was shared with racing legend Dale Earnhardt. His passing was very hard to take.

The seven-time NASCAR Winston Cup champion was solidly gunning for a record eighth championship when he fired his engine for the season-opening Daytona 500.

Sadly, Earnhardt would not take his last checkered flag on February 18, 2001. He would fall short of that mark some 500 yards after crashing in the fourth turn on the race's final lap.

Earnhardt's RCR Enterprises Chevrolet came to a stop after traveling from the bottom of turn four into the outside retaining wall. Fellow driver Ken Schrader made contact with Earnhardt's black and silver Chevrolet, turning Earnhardt more directly into the wall. Earnhardt's car finally came to a stop at the bottom of the turn, its front end heavily damaged from the crash. Drivers are told to drop the window net that protects them to indicate there is no injury. In this case, it never came down.

Schrader got out of his car and walked over to Earnhardt's driver-side window. Dropping the net, it was clear Earnhardt had suffered very serious injuries. Schrader began waving frantically for help, giving everyone an indication of how severe the situation was.

Earnhardt died of a blow to the head that caused a massive skull fracture, as well as a fracture to his sternum, eight fractured ribs on the left side and a fractured left ankle.

I had co-anchored the race that day and announced that third-place Earnhardt was in the wall as race winner Michael Waltrip and Dale Earnhardt Jr.—both in cars owned by Earnhardt crossed the finish line.

The hit Earnhardt endured looked routine from a distance, something I had seen many times during my career. The majority of the fans as well as those watching on television expected Earnhardt to come out of his car and greet his driver in victory lane. Those involved in the sport who saw the hit were deeply concerned. Direct head-on crashes are much worse than those spinning, end-over-end flips that look so dramatic.

I was deeply concerned and wanted to know Earnhardt's condition but was also afraid we would hear bad news. When I did get word, I wasn't prepared to hear it.

I could see the activity going on around Earnhardt's car by the rescue crews there on the scene. There was a feeling in the air that the outcome wasn't going to be good. An hour or so after the crash, Mike Helton, president of NASCAR, made the announcement that Earnhardt had been lost. After the official word confirmed he was gone, I think it was simply a blur for those of us in the media working on stories reporting the sad news of his death. We were all sort of going through the motions, all trying to absorb what we had just been told. It was one tough day to get through and every day since has had a feeling of something missing. I was just totally shocked. His death is still hard to talk about, even today.

When Earnhardt checked out, I just finally rationalized and made peace with myself, and with the Good Lord that it was simply Dale's time to go. It hurt me really, really bad when he died, and it still hurts and always will.

42

WHEN TO SAY GOODBYE

O ver the years, people have asked when I might do my final race broadcast and retire to the mountains around Elkin. That question remains to be answered. At 73, I still enjoy my work with MRN Radio and also enjoy the friendships in NASCAR's garage areas. I admit that due to the busy schedules the drivers endure today, it's difficult to cultivate the close friendships at the level enjoyed in the past. Plus, there is quite an age gap between me and some of today's drivers.

I still love to walk through the garage area and see and hear the cars. That part of it was the same in the 1950s as it is today. The crew works on the car and gets it ready for qualifying and for race day. The difference is there's a specialist for everything now where before you may have had a half-dozen guys on the crew of one of the top teams.

As I said before, it's tough nowadays to have relationships with any of the drivers because there's a vast age difference between, say, Kurt Busch, or some of the drivers younger than him, and me. I guess I've been more comfortable with drivers such as Ricky Rudd or the late Dale Earnhardt. I remember the first race they ever ran. I remember

Ricky came up in 1975 and I had a heck of a time saying, "Rookie Ricky Rudd."

As far as when I will step away, that's something I can't answer. I've thought about it a hundred times. Maybe at the end of a season, I may not say anything to anybody and just make up my mind and say to myself, "Barney, you're not going to be calling any more races." Or it may be that toward the end of December I say, "You need to get someone else to do it."

There are other times when I think I'd like to taper off and do maybe 15 races; I don't do the entire schedule now. That's a hard question to answer.

On occasion, I think about cutting my schedule back to a limited schedule. The travel can really burn you out. But I'm not quite ready for that yet, I don't think. I have to admit, I would really miss those who I've gotten to know over the years. I guess you could say those in the garage area are my family. We've spent so much time over the years and have enjoyed so many great friendships. And there have been sad times when some of those friends have passed away. Sometimes I look around and there are so many people who have been in the sport who are gone. There aren't that many of the early folks in the business around anymore, and that really bothers me. I sure do appreciate everyone who has helped me along the way, and there have been so many.

The 2005 season was my 47th year of covering races and following these things around. I still enjoy it and I love what I do on race day. I love to go in the booth and that's why I'm still in radio. In radio, you're saying what you see happening on the race track. If you want to talk about whose running 20th and why, you can do that, because that information will be interesting to someone. You can talk about the lead, what's going on in the pits or someone in the garage. You have the freedom to do that.

I just love radio. Radio is still fun.

Celebrate the Heroes of Auto Racing
in These Other Releases from Sports Publishing!